NAILING THE BAR

Simple
TORTS
Outline

Tim Tyler, Ph.D.
Attorney at Law

NINETY PERCENT of the LAW in NINETY PAGES. ®

Published by: ***Practical Step Press***
A Division of
LEGAL BOOKS DISTRIBUTING

--www.PracticalStepPress.com--

ISBN 978-1-936160-07-5

NINETY PERCENT of the LAW in NINETY PAGES.®

It takes thousands of pages to completely explain the law of **TORTS**. But such extensive knowledge is unnecessary to succeed in law school or on bar examinations.

This eBook gives a simple explanation of the common law of **TORTS** and broadly adopted modern rules for beginning law students, including **NEGLIGENCE** and **PRODUCT LIABILITY**. The purpose of this eBook is to provide law students with an **understanding** of the **basic law of torts** without a lot of unnecessary blather.

This eBook simply tells beginning law students the **BLACK LETTER LAW** and **BRIGHT LINE RULES** they need to know to succeed in law school. The explanation is given in **plain English** with the aid of **examples**. Other than that, this book deliberately avoids or minimizes discussion of case law and historical development.

The reason for this deliberate omission is that extensive discussion of case law, minority holdings and historical development is **UNNECESSARY** and often **more CONFUSING than helpful** to beginning law students trying to gain a basic understanding of the law.

YOUR PROFESSORS will probably focus on the details of the law in one or more narrow areas of their personal interest. Those details may not be covered in sufficient depth here. **As you realize a need for more detailed knowledge** in a particular and narrow area of law, consult an appropriate **hornbook from your library** or some other authoritative reference source.

OTHERWISE, THIS BOOK HAS ALL THAT YOU NEED to quickly understand the basic rules of law.

UNDERSTANDING THE LAW IS NECESSARY BUT NOT ENOUGH to succeed in law school! You must also be able to **explain** how the law applies to fact patterns presented on examinations.

THEREFORE, after you have developed an understanding of the law of contracts using this book, you MUST make additional efforts to prepare for your law school exams in contracts. To do that, use Nailing the Bar's **How to Write Essays for Torts Law School and Bar Exams (B), How to Write Essays for Contracts, UCC, Torts and Crimes Law School and Bar Exams (ABC) or Nailing the Baby Bar, How to Write Essays for the California First-Year Student Exam (BB).**

To test your knowledge and prepare for multiple-choice exams, use Nailing the Bar's **333 Multiple-Choice Questions for First-Year Law Students (MQ1).**

Table of Contents

Chapter 1: Tort Law Overview

This outline may not correspond exactly to the approach taken in your class work. The purpose here is to give you a logical explanation of the subject area, rather than to mirror any particular teaching approach.

A **TORT** is a wrongful act recognized by law as a "tort". An act is "wrongful" simply because English common law and English customs deem it to be wrongful. The "wrongful" act may be a breach of an existing duty to act. A person who commits a tort is a **tortfeasor**.

Tort actions are brought by **plaintiffs** who present a "**cause of action**" claiming the tortfeasor committed a tortuous act against them. There are many different tort causes of action. All of them require plaintiffs to prove certain **legal elements** by a **preponderance of the evidence**. A "preponderance" of evidence means the plaintiff must present more evidence or more convincing evidence than the defendant as to each element.

Many of the legal elements vary from one tort cause of action to another. But all torts share three common legal elements. Every tort action claims 1) the defendant has **acted wrongfully**, 2) that the wrongful act **caused** a wrongful result, and 3) that the plaintiff **deserves a remedy**.

Plaintiffs in a tort action have **no burden to prove they did not consent** to the tortuous acts of the defendant. Law students often incorrectly think this is something the plaintiff must prove. **Consent** is an **affirmative defense** that may be raised by the defendant in any tort action. If the defendant claims the plaintiff consented to the act complained of, the burden is on the defendant to prove it.

> **For example:** Brutus hits Caesar on the head with a baseball bat. There are no witnesses. If Brutus claims Caesar consented to be hit on the head, he has the burden of proving it. After all, if the burden was on Caesar to prove he did NOT consent to be hit on the head by a preponderance of the evidence it would be impossible because there are no witnesses and it would just be his word against Brutus. That is not a "preponderance" of evidence.

1. Tort Causes of Action

Tort causes of action may be divided into the following categories, and later the book will explain the details of these causes of action in this order:

1. **Strict Liability in Tort**
2. **Intentional Torts**
3. **Negligence**
4. **Products Liability**
5. **Defamation**
6. **Invasion of Privacy**
7. **Nuisance**
8. **Interference with Contract**
9. **Abuse of Process and Malicious Prosecution**
10. **Deceit, Nondisclosure and Negligent Misrepresentation**

2. Torts Distinguished from Crimes

Tort actions should not be confused with criminal prosecutions. Criminal actions are "**prosecutions**" while tort actions are "**civil actions**".

Prosecutions are "**criminal actions**" brought by and on behalf of **the State** against defendants who commit **wrongful acts against society**. In contrast, **tort actions** are "**civil actions**" brought by and on behalf of **plaintiffs** against defendants for **wrongful acts against the plaintiff**. The plaintiffs are usually private (non-government) parties, but that does not necessarily have to be true. A government agency can bring a tort action against a defendant the same as private parties.

The purpose of a **criminal action** is to punish "**criminals**" for **criminal acts**, not to be awarded a money judgment. The purpose of a **civil action** is to **obtain a money judgment** against the defendant to **compensate** the plaintiff **for damages**, to prevent the defendant from reaping **unjust enrichment** (legal restitution), and only occasionally to **financially punish** the defendant from wrongful acts in the future (exemplary damages).

The **burden of proof in a criminal action** is to prove each legal element of the crime **beyond a reasonable doubt**. The **criminal prosecution must always prove evil intent** or "mens rea". In contrast the **burden of proof in a tort action** is to prove each legal element by a **preponderance of the evidence**, and **evil intent never has to be proven** unless exemplary damages are sought.

Criminal defendants are found **"guilty"**. Tort defendants are "**liable**" but **never "guilty"**.

3. Right to a Jury Trial

Parties to <u>all</u> tort actions have a right to a jury trial. The right may be waived. The jury acts as the **finder of fact**. If a jury trial is waived the judge acts as the finder of fact. In either case the finder of fact decides whether the plaintiff has proven all of the required legal elements of the cause of action, and if so, the amount of money judgment the plaintiff deserves to be awarded as a remedy.

Chapter 2: Causation in Tort

Tort classes traditionally do not explain "causation" until negligence is discussed. But every tort plaintiff claims the defendant did "something wrong" that CAUSED a **tortuous result**. So "causation" is a basic claim in every tort action, and it is well to explain the rules of law for "causation" before detailed explanation of every possible tort cause of action. Causation often applies to <u>criminal analysis</u> too!

"Causation" is not as clear as it seems.

Plaintiffs who claim a tortfeasor **caused** a tortuous result must prove it in <u>all</u> tort causes of action. Usually the tortuous result is injury (damages) to the plaintiff, but it might also be unjust enrichment to the tortfeasor. The explanation below is often phrased in terms of injury and damages but the tortuous result can also be unjust enrichment in some situations.

Causation requires plaintiffs to prove the defendants' tortuous acts were the **actual cause of** or a **substantial factor** causing a tortuous result AND that they were the **proximate (legal cause)** as well.

1. Actual Causation

The tortuous act of a tortfeasor is the actual cause of the plaintiff's injury if the plaintiff would not have been injured **but for the defendant's act**. This is often called the "but for" test or the "sine qua non" test.

> **For Example:** Cheney is hunting and shoots his lawyer in the face. Cheney's act is the **actual cause** of the lawyer's injury because he would not have been injured **but for** Cheney shooting him in the face.

2. Substantial Factors

If two or more tortfeasors act wrongfully, and the plaintiff would not have been injured if none had acted wrongfully, but it can not be proven that the plaintiff would not have been injured **but for the wrongful behavior of each tortfeasor alone**, the act of each tortfeasor is a **substantial factor** in causing the plaintiff's injury.

> **For Example:** Cheney and Bush are hunting with Limbaugh and both shoot toward Limbaugh. One pellet hits Limbaugh in the eye. It cannot be proven whose pellet hit Limbaugh. So it cannot be proven that Limbaugh would not have been hurt **but for** the act of each defendant. But if neither of them had shot at Limbaugh he would not have been injured. Therefore, the act of each was a **substantial factor** in Limbaugh's injury.

The joint liability of two or more tortfeasors is explained in more detail in Chapter 4.

3. Proximate Causation

Plaintiffs in tort causes of action must ALSO prove the acts of the defendants were the **proximate** (or **legal**) **cause** of their injury. **Proximate cause** means the injury suffered by the plaintiff was the **foreseeable result of the defendant's act via an unbroken chain of causation that was so close in time and place** that the defendant should be held legally responsible for the result.

Another, equivalent way of stating this is that **proximate cause** means the results of an action are the **direct and natural consequences** the action. Or one could say an act is the proximate cause of the **foreseeable consequences** of that act. All of these statements mean the same thing.

--o0o--

A. Closeness in Time and Place

Although an act may be the actual cause of an injury, the more time that passes, the more chance there is that other events will occur that are also actual causes of the same injury. And after several different acts or events become additional "actual causes" of a result, the earlier and more distant acts and events are often disregarded as being the "proximate" cause of the result.

> **For Example:** Alice forgets to put gas in her car, and it stalls on the highway. Sam stops to help Alice, and he is late to work. Sam's boss, Bob, is unhappy and fires Bob. Bob can't pay his mortgage because he lost his job. Carl buys Bob's house in a foreclosure sale. A tornado destroys the house and kills Carl six years after Alice forgot to get gas. Carl would not have been killed **but for** Alice's negligence, because that started the whole chain of events. Alice is an actual cause of Carl's death, but if you were on the jury, would you conclude she killed Carl by forgetting to get gas?

--o0o--

B. Unforeseeable Intervening Events

For the chain of causation to be unbroken it **must not be interrupted** or **broken** by an **unforeseeable intervening event**. An unforeseeable intervening event is a **reasonably unforeseeable act by a third party** or an **act of God or nature** occurring after the defendant's wrongful act that is **also an actual cause** of the plaintiff's injury.

An event is **reasonably unforeseeable** to a defendant if it is improbable or unlikely. The fact that an event is "possible" does not make it probable or likely. It is possible you will win the lottery. But it is not very likely.

Here are two general rules of law, but be aware courts can rule contrary to these rules in certain circumstances.

1) Crimes and intentional torts by others are usually unforeseeable

Crimes and **intentional torts** are, by law, **unforeseeable acts** UNLESS defendants know, at the time they act, that <u>their acts are likely to cause</u> subsequent criminal acts or intentionally tortuous acts by others. So they are usually unforeseeable intervening events.

> **For Example:** Owen loans his car to Thirsty, knowing that he is drunk. Thirsty forgets to take the keys out of the car when he parks it. A thief sees the keys in the car, steals the car and drives it recklessly, crashing into Paula. Paula sues Owen and Thirsty for negligence. Are they liable? No. Paula would not have been injured **but for** the negligence of each of them, so Paula can prove **actual causation**. But the theft of the car by the "thief" was an unforeseeable intervening event, and it **breaks the chain of causation**. Paula cannot prove **proximate causation** and her case will fail.

2) Negligence by third parties is always foreseeable

Negligent acts by others are, by law, always **reasonably foreseeable** and are never unforeseeable intervening events.

> **For Example:** Cheney shoots his lawyer in the face. The lawyer is taken to the hospital. Suddenly an earthquake collapses the hospital and the lawyer is killed. The lawyer would not have died **but for** Cheney's act because he would not have been in the hospital otherwise. So Cheney's act is an **actual cause** of the lawyer's death. But the lawyer also would not have died **but for** the earthquake. So the earthquake is also an **actual cause** of the lawyer's death. And since the earthquake is an **unpredictable act of God** (or of nature if you prefer) that occurred **after** Cheney acted, it **broke the chain of causation**. Therefore, Cheney's act is **NOT the proximate cause** of the lawyer's death. Cheney is not liable.

--o0o--

C. Proximate Cause of Foreseeable Injury

If tortuous acts cause **foreseeable injuries** they generally are held to be the proximate cause of the injury, even though the injury occurs by an **unforeseeable sequence of events**.

> **For Example:** Dwayne negligently spills gasoline on the floor, cleans it up with rags, and puts the rags in a trash can. The trash is hauled away, but the rags catch fire by spontaneous combustion and the garbage truck is destroyed. Dwayne is the **proximate cause** of the fire because it was foreseeable his negligence could cause a fire.

--o0o--

D. Proximate Cause by Foreseeable Means

If tortuous acts cause injuries through a **foreseeable sequence of events** they generally are held to be the proximate cause of the injury, even though the type of injury is unforeseeable.

> **For Example:** Dwayne negligently spills gasoline on the floor, cleans it up with rags, and puts the rags in a trash can. Joe the janitor opens the can to get the trash, is overcome by the fumes, falls and bangs his head. Dwayne is the **proximate cause** of Joe's injury because it was foreseeable someone might be injured in other ways by the gasoline.

--o0o--

E. Unforeseeable Injury by Unforeseeable Means

When a tortuous act causes an **unforeseeable injury** through an **unforeseeable sequence of events**, it generally DOES break the chain of causation and the defendant is relieved of liability.

> **For Example:** Dwayne negligently spills gasoline, cleans it up, and flushes the rags down the toilet. Fumes from the gasoline set off an alarm at the Sewage Treatment Plant, shutting it down. The maintenance supervisor, Joe, rushes to the plant to see what the problem is, runs a stop sign and is injured in a collision. Joe's injury is an **unforeseeable injury** through an **unforeseeable sequence of events** and Dwayne is not going to be liable for that.

Chapter 3: Remedies in Tort

The **legal** remedy for <u>all</u> tort causes of action is **award of a money judgment**. Any other remedy is an **equitable** remedy and not a legal remedy. A legal remedy is one a plaintiff has a **right** to be awarded. An equitable remedy is one a Court has **discretion** to award. Nobody ever has a right to an equitable remedy. In tort law the only remedy a party has any **legal right** to be awarded is a money judgment.

If a money judgment is awarded by the Court, the party it is awarded to is the **judgment creditor**. In a tort situation the judgment creditor is always the **plaintiff** or a **cross-complainant**. The party who is liable for the money judgment is the **judgment debtor**. In a tort situation that will always be the **defendant** or a **cross-defendant**. It is possible for the Court to issue a judgment against the initial plaintiff who is a cross-defendant on a cross-complaint filed by the original defendant.

There are <u>three possible reasons</u> a Court will award a money judgment in tort. First, if tortfeasors caused plaintiffs to suffer **injuries** (damages), the plaintiffs have a **legal right** to a money judgment <u>to compensate</u> them for those injuries. This is called an **award of damages**. Damage awards are **always** awarded to **plaintiffs**.

Second, if tortfeasors have **reaped an unjust enrichment** by their wrongful behavior, the plaintiffs have a **legal right** to a money judgment <u>to prevent unjust enrichment</u> to the tortfeasor. This is called an **award of legal restitution**. In odd cases awards of legal restitution may actually be awarded to a defendant, even though the defendant is the tortfeasor.

Third, if tortfeasors have acted with **malice, oppression** and **fraud**, the plaintiffs have a legal right to a money judgment to <u>punish</u> the tortfeasors for their wrongful behavior. This is called an **award of exemplary** or **punitive damages**, but it is less confusing to call them **punitive awards**.

A tortfeasor will never be awarded a money judgment by the Court because torts are wrongful acts, and the Court will never reward a person for wrongful acts. However, if both parties to an action have committed torts against each other, the Court may award one a judgment on a finding that they have suffered more injury (or reaped less unjust enrichment) than the other party.

It is traditional to say that plaintiffs in tort actions have the burden of proving "**damages**". But that is not exactly true. Plaintiffs must actually prove they have a **right to a remedy**, but in the vast majority of situations that means they must prove they suffered damages as a result of the defendants' wrongful acts. In the remaining minority of cases plaintiffs might prove instead that the defendants have reaped an **unjust enrichment** from their wrongful acts.

Although the basis for the vast majority of tort judgments is **damages** suffered by the plaintiff, you should always remember legal restitution is always an alternative possibility.

If a money judgment is an inadequate remedy the Court has **discretion** to grant plaintiffs **equitable remedies** such as **injunctive relief**. But nobody has a "right" to an equitable remedy.

1. Damages

In all tort cases **damages** are the <u>money measure</u> of injuries the wrongful acts of the tortfeasor cause the plaintiff. Tort **damages** are calculated as **sum of two amounts** called **special damages** and **general damages**. These may be called "regular damages" to distinguish them from "punitive" or "exemplary" damages which are an entirely different thing.

--o0o--

A. Special Damages

In tort law **special damages** are the **monetary losses** the tortuous act of the tortfeasor caused the plaintiff. They are often "out of pocket" expenses like medical bills, others are expenses to replace or repair damaged property, whether that is done or not, and others are to compensate for lost profits and wages in either the past or future. These are generally called **out-of-pocket** damages.

> **For Example:** Tom hits Dick in an auto accident, and Dick is hospitalized as a result. Dick's **medical bill** is $10,000. Dick proves he had $5,000 in **lost wages** while in the hospital. He proves his car was destroyed, so he had **property damages** of $2,000. His expert witness estimates the **present value** of his **lost future wages** will be $200,000. Based on these finding Dick may be awarded a judgment for $217,000. These would be **special damages** because it is to compensate Dick for his **actual monetary losses**.

1) Property damage

Lost or destroyed property is valued at **fair market value**, and damages to property are valued at **repair cost**, but generally only up to a **maximum of fair market value.**

Items of sentimental value that have no market value cannot be valued based on sentimental value alone, but some Court's have allowed damages for **objective sentimental value**. This is not the general rule.

2) Economic losses caused by property damage

Plaintiffs may recover economic damages in a tort action (e.g. lost profits, lost wages) directly caused by the defendant's damage to property IF the **plaintiff had a proprietary interest in the property damaged**. But traditionally he would not otherwise have standing to pursue a claim. The economic damages must be provable and unavoidable.

> **For Example:** Tom deliberately burns down Dick's rice mill. Dick loses $1 million in profits because he is unable to fulfill rice milling contracts. And Harry, a rice farmer, loses $100,000 because he cannot sell his rice to Dick's mill as he had expected. Generally, Dick can recover his lost profits because he had a **proprietary interest** in the mill. But Harry generally cannot recover because he only had an **expectancy** that he would profit from the mill rather than a proprietary interest.

3) Economic losses caused by breach of contract

Plaintiffs generally cannot recover economic damages caused by a **total failure** to perform contract duties in a tort action; generally, the remedy is in contract law. An **exception** is recognized for a **nonfeasance** by a public utility or regulated common carrier.

Plaintiffs may be able to recover economic damages caused by **negligent or deliberate PARTIAL failure** to perform contract duties in a tort action **by those the contract was intended to benefit**.

> **For Example:** Pricey-Watergate, an accounting firm, is hired by Lemon Brothers, an investment bank, to file all reports required by the SEC. Pricey-Watergate fails to file the necessary reports and Lemon Brothers is barred from trading on the major exchanges. Since the purpose of the contract was to protect Lemon Brothers, the firm may bring a tort action against Pricey-Watergate for its lost profits.

4) Personal injury

Personal injury will be based on past and projected future 1) **medical costs**, 2) **lost income** and 3) **pain and suffering**. Pain and suffering are **general damages** as explained below.

5) Egg-shell plaintiffs

Defendants that are extremely vulnerable to injury, <u>through no fault of their own</u>, are called **"egg-shell" plaintiffs**.

If defendants breach their duties and thereby actually and proximately cause injury to any plaintiff, then the defendants are liable for ALL the injuries caused, even if amount, type and extent of injury suffered by the plaintiff is **<u>totally unforeseeable</u>** by the defendants at the time of the negligent act. [1] (See *Bartolone v. Jeckovich* (1984) 481 N.Y.2d 545.)

The catch phrase used to explain this is "<u>a defendant must take his plaintiff as he finds him</u>."

> **For Example:** Clumsy bumps into Vick by accident. Vick, a hemophiliac, gets a tiny bruise. But it grows worse, causing him to be hospitalized for several weeks. Clumsy is liable for the entire hospital bill and all of Vick's lost wages, pain and suffering, etc.

The concept of "egg-shell" plaintiff does not extend to plaintiffs that help cause their own injury through their own intentional or negligent acts. When plaintiffs intentionally do things that cause themselves injury they are said to have **assumed the risk** of injury. And if plaintiffs negligently do things that cause them injury they are said to have been **contributorily** or **comparatively negligent**. Those defenses to negligence are explained below.

> **For Example:** Driver causes a very minor auto accident. Vick is seriously injured because he was not wearing his seatbelt, in violation of traffic laws. Vick is not an "egg-shell" plaintiff because his vulnerability to injury was substantially caused by his own negligence.

---

[1] Of course, the same concept applies to injuries arising from intentional torts as well.

6) Physical injury caused by fright alone

Modernly the majority view is a negligent defendant is liable for **physical injuries** caused **indirectly** by fright alone.

> **For Example:** Driver almost hits (but misses) Vick with his car. Vick faints and hits his head. In the most jurisdictions Driver is liable for Vick's injury. A minority of Courts holds that Driver is not liable unless he actually touched Vick with the car.

--o0o--

B. General Damages

In tort law **general damages** are a money judgment awarded to compensate the plaintiff for **non-monetary injuries** such as **pain, emotional distress**, **disfigurement**, **loss of consortium** (deprivation of companionship, sexual intercourse, etc), and **inconvenience**. They are generally called **pain and suffering**.

> **For Example:** Tom hits Dick in an auto accident, and Dick is hospitalized as a result. Dick shows the jury his scars and tells how painful his injuries were. He tells how he was unable to have sexual intercourse for a year, and as a result his wife ran off with a door-to-door vacuum salesman. His expert witnesses say he now has an inferiority complex and will be troubled for years to come. The finder of fact may or may not believe this. If he is awarded some amount for these injuries it is called **general damages**.

The tort plaintiff has a legal right to award of a money judgment equal to the SUM of the special and general damages the finder of fact concludes the plaintiff has suffered.

1) Mental distress alone

Under early common law damages for mental distress (e.g. nervousness, irritability, loss of sleep) often could NOT be recovered unless the plaintiff could also prove some **physical injuries**. Nevertheless, "shock" to the nervous system (as in the phrase "she went into shock") was considered a physical injury because it is a physical manifestation of mental distress.

Modernly this requirement has been eliminated or substantially relaxed. Generally, damages for negligence can be awarded for mental distress alone as long as it is sufficiently manifested to prove injury has occurred (e.g. testimony that the defendant exhibited hysteria, insomnia, depression, withdrawal, etc.)

2) Loss of consortium

Under common law a husband could recover for **loss of consortium** because of injury to a wife, if the wife suffered sufficient injury to maintain an independent action. Modernly wives may also recover for loss of consortium in many jurisdictions for injuries to husbands.

2. Legal Restitution

The plaintiff in all tort actions has a **legal right** to request award of a money judgment for **legal restitution** instead of an award of **damages**. Legal restitution means a money judgment calculated to prevent the defendant from **enjoying an unjust enrichment** from his wrongful act. However, in many tort actions the defendants have enjoyed no enrichment at all or else the damages suffered by the plaintiffs far exceed the gains enjoyed by the defendants. Therefore, tort actions seek an award of damages far more often than they seek an award of legal restitution.

An award of legal restitution may be called "restitutionary damages" but that is just a confusing idea. It is far better to call this "legal restitution" and leave the idea of "damages" out of it.

Legal restitution is **awarded as an alternative** to an award of damages. The plaintiff cannot be awarded both amounts. Plaintiffs who are awarded legal restitution are said to have "**waived the tort**". But the plaintiff can plead for both remedies, and leave it to the finder of fact to determine which amount is the larger.

> **For Example:** Booker embezzles $1,000 from Company and uses it to gamble. He wins $100,000 in a poker tournament and puts the $1,000 back. Company can sue him for **trespass to chattel**. But it has not suffered any **damages** at all. So if Company sues for damages, it gets nothing. But it has a legal right to be awarded the $100,000 Booker won as **legal restitution** to prevent him from enjoying an unjust enrichment.

3. Punitive Awards

If plaintiffs prove defendants acted with **malice, fraud** or **oppression** they may have a **legal right** to an award of a money judgment as a **punitive** measure. These are traditionally called "**punitive damages**" or "**exemplary damages**" because they "make an example" of the defendant.

Punitive awards are not intended to compensate plaintiffs for the actual injury they have suffered, so calling them "**punitive damages**" is confusing. Plaintiffs do not have to prove they suffered "regular damages" to deserve an award of punitives, and punitive awards might be awarded precisely because the plaintiffs cannot prove they suffered much "actual" injury. To minimize this confusion I will call them "**punitive awards**" or "**punitives**" rather than "damages", but you should understand they traditionally are called "punitive damages".

> **For Example:** Darren kidnaps Bambi to take her to his mountain hideout to be his "sex slave". But after 3 minutes Bambi jumps out of his car, escapes and calls the police. Darren is arrested and sentenced to prison for kidnapping. Bambi sues Darren for false imprisonment, but admits she did not suffer much any "injury" during the 3 minutes she was confined. The Court (e.g. jury) may award her **nominal** damages for the injury she actually suffered (e.g. $1) and a $10,000 **punitive award** to punish Darren for his acts.

Punitives can be awarded in addition to an award of "regular damages or an award of legal restitution. They are an additional remedy, not an alternative remedy.

Punitives are **never awarded for negligent acts**, unless there is proof of **gross negligence** or **recklessness**.

Gross negligence means causing the plaintiff injury by **deliberately breaching an existing duty** to protect the plaintiff from extreme risks. The deliberateness of the breach, as compared to an accidental breach, is what makes it "gross" negligence and not "regular" negligence.

> **For Example:** Nurse agrees to care for Ima, an invalid. Ima develops severe bed sores, but out of spite and malice Nurse deliberately does nothing to treat her. That is gross negligence, and Ima may have a right to a punitive award in addition to an award of "regular" damages.

Recklessness means causing the plaintiff injury by **deliberately creating extreme risks** to the plaintiff. Here again the deliberateness of creating the risks as opposed to accidentally creating dangers is what makes this "recklessness" and not "regular" negligence.

> **For Example:** Bubba engages in a drag race on a public street. Since he deliberately created risks to bystanders he was "recklessness".

The right to a punitive award is usually defined in statute and the decision whether to award punitives, and how much the punitive award should be is heavily dependent on the finder of fact. But if the finder of fact determines the defendant acted with malice, oppression or fraud, AND that an award of punitives is appropriate to punish and deter the defendant, THEN the plaintiff has a legal right to the award.

Punitive awards **cannot be excessive** because the 8th Amendment prohibits "excessive fines" and "cruel and unusual punishments". Punitive awards must be **reasonable**.

To be reasonable, the amount of a punitive award should reflect:

1) The **seriousness of the harm** posed by the defendant's acts;
2) The defendant's **deliberateness in causing the harm**;
3) The defendant's **awareness of the harm** being caused;
4) The **duration** of the defendant's harmful acts;
5) The **unnecessary nature** of the defendant's harmful acts;
6) The **level of regulatory control** over the defendant's harmful acts;
7) The **length of time since** the defendant's harmful acts;
8) The **wealth** of the defendant; and
9) The **amount of other claims** that have been filed against the defendant.

4. Collateral Source Rule

Under the **Collateral Source Rule** evidence of insurance proceeds, remarriage, windfalls, and other mitigation of damages suffered by plaintiffs is inadmissible evidence to reduce or increase liability.

5. Equitable Remedies

If a money judgment would be an inadequate remedy a judge (not a jury) has discretion to award **equitable remedies**. The judge may also award equitable relief as an interim measure or temporary remedy to prevent a moving party from suffering irreparable harm before trial of a dispute. The party that "moves" for a remedy is called the **movant** and the other party the **respondent**. Sometimes the defendant in a tort action is the movant seeking an equitable remedy.

The judge may order that certain property be conveyed to the movant or held in trust for the movant. When specific property is involved or specific equitable remedies are sought this may be called "**specific relief**". A court order telling a respondent to do or not do some act is often called **injunctive relief** or an "**injunction**".

The Court (judge) has **discretion** to grant an equitable remedy, but movants have no "right" to receive them.

5. Collecting on the Judgment

Tort plaintiffs who are awarded money judgments are **judgment creditors** and the tortfeasors are **judgment debtors**. The burden is on judgment creditors to **collect** on the judgments by means set forth in State statutes. After the Court issues the money judgment it has no further involvement. This is true without regard to whether the judgment is issued for **damages** suffered, as **legal restitution** to prevent unjust enrichment, as **punitive awards**, or as an **equitable remedy** (equitable restitution).

State collection procedures vary, but typically judgment creditors file an **abstract of judgment** with County Recorders to create automatic liens on any real property owned by the judgment debtors in that County. Then they obtain a **writ of execution** to have the County Sheriff sell the judgment debtor's real property at a Sheriff's sale to satisfy the judgment. Judgment creditors can also get a **writ of attachment** and have the County Sheriff seize personal property of the judgment debtors such as cars and boats to be sold at a Sheriff's sale. Judgment creditors can also **garnish** the wages of the judgment debtors.

But in many cases judgment debtors are penniless losers. In that case judgment creditors cannot collect on their money judgments and they are just worthless pieces of paper.

A money judgment is the standard tort remedy and is not considered by a Court of law to be an "inadequate remedy" simply because the judgment creditor is unable to collect on it.

Chapter 4: Liability in Tort

All torts are subject to the same rules of liability. Defendants who commit tortuous acts against plaintiffs are generally **directly liable** to the plaintiffs. But there are particular rules for different situations.

1. Survival of Claims

Under common law the death of either the plaintiff or the defendant terminated all tort claims. Modernly, **survival statutes** allow some tort claims to continue after the death of the parties.

Generally, **liability for general damages is terminated by the death** of a plaintiff, but liability for special damages is not.

Some State statutes allow some general damages to be awarded after the death of a plaintiff. For example, in California statutes create a statutory cause of action for **elder abuse**, and death of the plaintiff (the elderly person) does not release defendants from liability for general damages.

2. Liability for Wrongful Death

Claims for **wrongful death** are based on statutes and may allow **parties with standing** to recover for loss of income and companionship. A wrongful death suit is a claim that the plaintiff suffered a loss (e.g. a loss of income, consortium, companionship, etc.) because the defendant caused the death of another person. This is a theory of liability, not a cause of action. For example, the cause of action may be negligence, an intentional tort, or strict liability.

Modernly most Courts hold that **parents** have a right to bring wrongful death suits if **their children are born dead** due to the negligence of the defendant even though child was never a living person.

Damages in wrongful death suits are substantially based on **actuarial estimates** of the **expected life span** of the decedent, their **expected future income**, and the amounts of that income the plaintiffs would have received if the decedent had not been killed by the acts of the defendants.

> **For Example:** Granny is 95 years old, suffering severe dementia, and living in a nursing home. Her sole source of income is Social Security, and it pays for part of her care. The Welfare Department pays for the rest of the expenses of her care. Granny accidentally dies when she is given the wrong medication. Daughter sues for wrongful death. Since Daughter did not receive any income from Granny, and would not have received any in the future, she has no basis for claiming a monetary loss. And since Granny suffered severe dementia, and no doubt had a very short life expectancy, there is not a very good basis for claiming loss of companionship either.

3. Tort Actions Involving Children

--o0o--

A. Liability to Parents for Injuries to Their Children

Under common law an action could be brought by parents **on their own behalf** against others for injuries caused to their minor children. The basis for the claim was that it caused them **loss of labor services** by the child.

Modernly courts generally reject this cause of action on the ground that the injury has been to the child and not to the parent. However, the child can bring an action in his own right for his or her injuries, and the parent may bring the suit **as guardian ad litem on behalf of the child.**

Nevertheless, a parent may bring an action for the **wrongful death** of a child as explained above.

--o0o--

B. Liability of Parents to Children for Their Injury

Children can bring actions against parents for acts causing injury to the child. This is a very common situation. The parent often instigates the action for the child so that the child can collect from the parent's insurance company.

> **For Example:** Bevis negligently causes an auto accident which injures his son, Junior. For Junior to collect damages from Bevis' insurance carrier, Bevis and Junior's mother, Bambi, agree that she will file a claim against Bevis for negligence on behalf of Junior as his guardian ad litem. Bevis, of course, admits he was negligent, Junior "wins", and Bevis' insurance company must pay for his injuries.

A negligence action may be brought against a parent on behalf of a child for **failure to properly supervise the child**.

> **For Example:** Bevis has physical custody of his son, Junior, for the weekend under a divorce agreement. He has a duty, as a parent, to act reasonably to protect his child. Bevis fails to watch Junior and he wanders into the street where he is run over by a car. Junior's mother, Bambi, can file a suit for Junior against Bevis for his injuries on the basis of negligence.

But generally NO claim may be maintained that the parent caused **psychological damage** by **generally failing** to properly exercise parental discretion or by failing to provide a nurturing or advantageous childhood. In other words, children can sue parents for physical injuries but not for just being a "bad" parent.

--o0o--

C. Liability of Parents to Children for Giving Birth

Generally, "wrongful life" claims brought **against parents** by **children with birth defects** on the argument the parent **was aware** of the birth defect and **was negligent for not aborting** the pregnancy have been REJECTED by the Courts.

--o0o--

D. Liability of Physicians to Children for Their Birth

Generally, Courts have NOT held in favor of **children with birth defects** bringing claims against medical professionals claiming that **medical negligence** caused them to be born (because otherwise if the parents had been warned of the birth defect the pregnancy would have been aborted).

Some Courts have found in favor of such plaintiffs with damage awards limited to special damages and extraordinary expenses.

--o0o--

E. Liability of Physicians to Parents for Birth of Child

Generally, a growing number of "wrongful birth" claims have been supported by the Courts. These are brought **by parents against medical professionals** on claims that negligence by the physician caused the birth of a child that was **never wanted** or **would not have been wanted** but for the physician's negligence. These are either claims that the medical professional failed to act responsibly to prevent birth (e.g. a bungled vasectomy) or failed to act reasonably to discover and inform the parent about fetal birth defects that would have resulted in abortion of the fetus.

Courts are divided on damages awarded.

4. Liability of Co-Defendants

When plaintiffs are awarded money judgments based on tort causes of action against co-defendants they may be **joint tortfeasors**, **concurrent tortfeasors**, **successive tortfeasors**, or some may be **vicariously liable** for the tortuous acts of others.

- **Joint tortfeasors** are co-defendants that **act together**, in concert, to cause the plaintiff's injury.
- **Concurrent tortfeasors** are co-defendants whose **independent acts** coincidentally cause an **indivisible injury** to the plaintiff.
- **Successive tortfeasors** are defendants whose **independent acts** cause **two successive injuries** to the plaintiff such that the act of the **second tortfeasor aggravates** the injury caused by the first tortfeasor.
- **Vicariously liable defendants** are those who have committed no tortuous acts at all. Rather their liability arises from their **relationship** to the co-defendant who is **directly liable**.

--o0o--

A. Liability of Joint and Concurrent Tortfeasors

Traditionally, **joint** and **concurrent tortfeasors** are **jointly and severally liable** to the plaintiff. This means that **EACH alone may be forced to pay for ALL of the plaintiff's injury**.

There are **three situations** when joint and several liability is normally imposed:

1. When two or more tortfeasors **acted together** (acted "in concert") to injure the plaintiff (e.g. Bevis holds Vick while Butthead kicks him);
2. When two or more tortfeasors all **breached a common duty** to the plaintiff (e.g. Daddy and Mommy both fail to feed their child, Vick); and
3. When two or more tortfeasors act independently but cause **indivisible harm** to the plaintiff (e.g. Tom is driving recklessly when Barbara negligently pulls in front of him without looking. Their cars collide and crash into Dick. The injury to Dick cannot be separated into portions caused by the negligence of each defendant alone).

The plaintiff can collect the full amount of the damage award from any co-defendant, but the defendants are equally liable. When a plaintiff collects on a money judgment from any jointly and severally liable co-defendant, that defendant has a right to a contribution from the other jointly and severally liable co-defendants. The right to contribution may also be called a right of "reimbursement" or "indemnification", but "indemnification" really means the right of defendants who are only vicariously liable to fully recover from defendants who are directly liable. The burden is on defendants to recover reimbursement from the other co-defendants in the same manner the burden is on a plaintiff to collect on judgments against any co-defendant.

> **For Example:** Tom wins a damage award of $100,000 against Dick and Harry who are held to be jointly and severally liable. Dick owns a house but Harry is homeless. So Tom collects the $100,000 from Dick by placing a lien on his real property and having the Sheriff sell it on the Courthouse steps. Dick has the right to seek indemnity in the amount of $50,000 from Harry. Good luck, Dick.

1) Effect of release of one co-defendant alone

Under the common law if the plaintiff entered into a **release** against one co-defendant, all co-defendants were released from liability. Modernly a settlement with one co-defendant is seen as a **covenant not to sue** rather than a release of all claims, and the plaintiff can pursue claims against the other co-defendants.

> **For Example:** Tom wins a damage award of $90,000 against Dick and Harry who are held to be jointly and severally liable, with Dick found to be 2/3 responsible for Tom's injury and Harry to be 1/3 responsible. Harry offers to pay Tom $30,000 if he will release him from further liability. If they reach a settlement Tom can still seek recovery from Dick under the more modern view.

2) Right of co-defendant to contribution

Traditionally a joint or concurrent tortfeasor that paid a money judgment to a plaintiff could NOT seek reimbursement from the other tortfeasors, but modernly, a **tortfeasor** may seek **contribution** from other tortfeasors. Modernly "contribution" and "indemnity" have identical meaning.

Contribution is required by **equal division** unless states have applied a rule of **comparative fault** to contribution. Then contribution is in the proportion of the **relevant fault** of the parties.

> **For Example:** Tom wins a damage award of $90,000 against Dick and Harry. Dick was found to be 2/3 responsible for Tom's injury, and Harry to be 1/3 responsible. Harry pays Tom $30,000. Harry has a right to contribution from Dick. In some states he has a right to recover $15,000 (half) and in others he has a right to recover $20,000 (two-thirds).

3) Right to contribution from settling co-defendant

If one concurrent tortfeasor settles a dispute the other concurrent tortfeasors **may or may not be barred** from seeking reimbursement from the settling defendant, depending on jurisdiction.

> **For Example:** Tom and Dick are concurrent tortfeasors against Harry, and Harry settles his claim against Tom for $10,000. The court later finds at trial that Harry's damages are $100,000 and that Tom and Dick were equally at fault. Under the rules of joint and several liability Dick must pay Harry $90,000 ($100,000 less $10,000 already received). In some jurisdictions Dick can obtain reimbursement from Tom for $40,000. In other jurisdictions Dick is barred from obtaining reimbursement because public policy is to encourage settlement.

--o0o--

B. Liability of Successive Tortfeasors

Successive tortfeasors are defendants whose **independent acts** cause **two successive injuries** to the plaintiff such that the act of the **second tortfeasor aggravates** the injury caused by the first tortfeasor. Typically, the first tortfeasor is liable for **all** of the injury while the second is only liable for the **additional** injury caused. However, the first tortfeasor can seek **indemnity for all injury caused by the second tortfeasor**.

> **For Example:** Tom injures Dick in an accident causing $100,000 worth of injury. Dick is rushed to the hospital where Dr. Harry commits medical malpractice, causing Dick another $50,000 in damages. Dick's total injury is $150,000. Tom and Dr. Harry are **successive tortfeasors** because they independently caused successive injuries. But Tom is liable for **all** of Dick's injuries because Dick would not have been injured by Dr. Harry if he had not first been injured by Dick. But, Dr. Harry is **only liable** for the **additional** injury he caused, $50,000. If Tom pays Dick the entire $150,000, he can seek indemnity from Harry for $50,000.

--o0o--

C. Vicariously Liable Co-Defendants

Defendants who are not **directly liable** for tortuous acts may be **vicariously liable** if a **special relationship** exists between the defendants, and that is not so simple. Some typical relationships that may give rise to vicarious liability are:

- Employer-Employee
- Principal-Agent
- Master-Servant
- Business partners
- Joint Enterprise

Generally, defendants are vicariously liable for the tortuous acts of others only if the acts are committed **within the express or implied course and scope** of their special relationship, AND the person who actually commits the tort (the tortfeasor) has **less or equal control**. In other words, parties in a relationship that have less control than the tortfeasor are not vicariously liable for the acts of the tortfeasor.

> **For example:** Boss hires Worker as his employee. Boss rapes a customer in the store. Worker is not liable for that because he is the employee, not the employer, and as an employee he has less control than Boss, the tortfeasor.

Defendants with vicarious liability are co-defendants the same as co-defendants with direct liability.

1) Doctrine of respondeat superior

Under the doctrine of **RESPONDEAT SUPERIOR, employers** are liable for all tort injuries caused to others by their **employees** if the employees are **acting within the scope of their employment relationship**. It does not matter if the tort injury is intentional or accidental.

The same principal applies to master-servant and principal-agent relationships. **Principals** (masters) are liable for all torts inflicted on others by **agents** (servants) if the agents are **acting within the scope of their agency relationship** at the time. That means they are "**on the job**" when they inflict injury on the plaintiff. The fact that they were not supposed to injure anyone or were misbehaving is totally irrelevant.

> **For example:** Boss hires Worker to sell vacuum cleaners door-to-door. Worker calls on Buffy in her home to sell her a vacuum. He rapes her instead. Boss is liable for Buffy's injuries because Worker did this during a "sales visit". That means he acted within the scope of employment even though he was not supposed to rape the customers.

But if the employee (or agent or servant) leaves the workplace or begins engaging in activities that have nothing to do with the purpose of their employment (or agency or service) then they will be deemed to be on a "**frolic and detour**" and not acting within the scope of employment (or agency or service). In this case the employer (or principal or master) will not be vicariously liable.

For example: Boss hires Worker to sell door-to-door. Instead of selling door-to-door, Worker goes to a bar, gets drunk and punches Bob in the nose. Boss is not liable to Bob because Worker was on a "frolic and detour" when Bob was injured.

2) Vicarious joint enterprise liability

A **joint enterprise** is an agreement between two or more parties to work together for **mutual benefit** in a venture in which the parties have **equal voice and control**. It is also called "**joint venture**". A common situation is a business partnership, but "**joint enterprise**" often implies an agreement that is narrower than many general partnerships.

Each member of a joint enterprise is vicariously liable for all tortuous acts of the other participants **if they are committed within the scope** of the enterprise agreement.

For Example: Dewey, Cheatum and Howe are law partners. Dewey steals the clients' trust funds and goes to Mexico. Cheatum and Howe are liable because it is a joint venture.

A **joint enterprise** is often of **limited duration and scope** and extends to activities for **mutual benefit** other than purely profit. But **all participants must have equal voice and control** over the activities or "instrumentalities" that cause injury to others.

For Example: Tom and Dick agree to drive Tom's car to Chicago, sharing expenses and driving duties along the way. Tom deliberately rams Harry's car in a fit of road rage. Dick is not vicariously liable for the act of Tom on the basis of joint enterprise because it was Tom's car. Tom could have made Dick get out of the car at any time. If Dick did not have equal voice and control it is not a joint venture.

3) Vicarious liability of auto owners

Some states hold auto owners vicariously liable for any negligence by **ANY driver given permission** to drive the car. Other states hold under the **FAMILY PURPOSE RULE** that a car owner is only vicariously liable for negligence by **FAMILY MEMBERS given permission** to drive the car.

These rules of vicarious liability for automobiles vary considerably by State. [2]

But even if a car owner is not vicariously liable, they may ALWAYS be found directly liable if they loan their car someone **no reasonable person would allow** having the car.

4) No vicarious liability for parents

Parents are NOT generally vicariously liable for the **tortuous acts of their children**, but this may be modified by statute.

---

[2] In California for example the owner of any car is vicariously liable for negligence by anyone who is given permission to drive the car up to the minimum auto liability limits set by law. The owner is not vicariously liable above that level, but could be directly liable for negligent entrustment.

Parents may be **directly liable** for their OWN negligence in failing to **control** the child if the parent knows the child presents a likely danger to others.

And, parents may be **directly liable** for their OWN negligence for **negligent entrustment** if they provide the child with a **dangerous instrumentality** (e.g. a gun) that causes injury to others.

> **For Example:** Paula's little boy, Sonny, burns down Neighbor's house. Paula is not vicariously liable for Sonny's act. But she may be directly liable for negligent entrustment if she gave Sonny the matches, OR if she knew Sonny is a pyromaniac and did nothing to stop him.

5) Vicarious liability for acts of independent contractors

People who enter into contracts with **independent contractors** are not vicariously liable for torts committed by the contractors **unless their duty was non-delegable**.

Independent contractors generally provide **narrowly prescribed services** in exchange for payment, **are not supervised** by the persons receiving the services, are **substantially free to make independent decisions** concerning service delivery, and are **free to provide services to several parties** at the same time.

> **For Example:** Paula hires Charley Manson to clean her house once a week. Charley kills Paula's guests. Paula is not vicariously liable because Charley's an independent contractor.

Some duties are **non-delegable**, and people who enter into contracts with independent contractors ARE vicariously liable for torts they commit. Duties are non-delegable when:

- The activity involved is **highly dangerous** (e.g. blasting); OR
- The duties are based on **relationship** (e.g. duties of a parent, attorney, doctor, landlord, etc.).

> **For Example:** Larry Lawyer agrees to represent client Carl. He delegates his duties to his associate, Arnie Alcoholic. Arnie fails to file the necessary pleadings and Carl's complaint is time barred. Larry is vicariously liable for Arnie's neglect because the duty of an attorney to the client is non-delegable.

6) Vicariously liable defendant's right to full indemnity

Defendants that are only **vicariously liable** have a right to **full indemnity** from co-defendants that are **directly liable** for all amounts paid against the judgment. Vicarious liability is explained below.

> **For Example:** Worker is employed by Boss. Worker negligently injures Paula while acting within the scope of his employment. Worker is **directly liable** and Boss is **vicariously liable**. Paula is issued $10,000 damage award. If Boss pays Paula the $10,000 judgment he has a **right to full reimbursement** of $10,000 from Worker.

Chapter 5: Strict Liability Causes of Action

Strict liability is a distinct type of negligence **cause of action**. If the defendant engages in specified activities both duty and breach are presumed if the plaintiff can prove causality and damages. The cause of action should be pled as "negligence based on strict liability."

Tort defendants are strictly liable to plaintiffs for any injury caused by their participation in **four inherently dangerous activities** if the **injury is caused by the inherent dangers** of those activities. This is called **strict liability in tort**. The five activities are:

- Keeping **known dangerous pets**;
- Keeping **exotic animals**;
- Keeping **animals likely to roam**;
- Engaging in **abnormally dangerous** or **ultra-hazardous activities**.

1. Keeping Known Dangerous Pets

Defendants who keep a pet that is known to have dangerous proclivities are strictly liable to any plaintiff that is injured because of those proclivities. The most common "pet" in this regard is a dog.

Defendants are only strictly liable if they know the pet is dangerous. It is often said the "first bite is free", meaning that the owner is not strictly liable until after the pet has bitten someone because until then the owner does not know the pet is dangerous

Animals that may be dangerous but are not "pets" like bulls, horses and honeybees are not "known dangerous pets".

The injury to the plaintiff must be because of the animal's dangerous proclivities, not some unrelated characteristic.

> **For Example:** Owen's dog snaps at his house guests and kills several neighborhood cats. One day Owen's guest Peter trips over the dog as it is sleeping in the doorway and breaks his leg. Owen is not strictly liable because Peter was not injured by the dog's dangerous characteristics.

2. Keeping Exotic Animals

Defendants who keep exotic animals for any reasons are strictly liable to any plaintiff injured by the peculiar characteristics of the animal, including being frightened by it, whether the animal appears to be dangerous or not. Exotic animals are those that are not commonly domesticated.

> **For Example:** Owen keeps an old Lion that is as gentle as a lamb. One day a deliveryman comes to Owen's house, is frightened by the Lion and has a heart attack. Owen IS strictly liable for the deliveryman's injury because one of the "inherent dangers' of keeping an animal of this nature is that it will frighten people.

3. Keeping Animals Likely to Roam

Under the common law defendants who keep domesticated animals that are likely to roam unless confined to a fenced area, are strictly liable to any plaintiff that is injured because the animals get loose and roam about the area. This general rule is often modified by State statutes.

The injury to the plaintiff must be because of the roaming nature of the animals, not some unrelated characteristic.

> **For Example:** Farmer has a heard of cows. One day a storm blows down his fence and the cows roam onto the roadway. Driver accidentally runs into the cows and is badly injured. Farmer is strictly liable for Driver's injuries.

4. Abnormally Dangerous and Ultra-Hazardous Activities

Defendants engaging in "abnormally dangerous" or "ultra-hazardous" activities are strictly liable for injuries caused to others. Under early English law these were called "abnormally dangerous" activities and modernly they are often called "ultra-hazardous" activities. There is no clearly recognized distinction between the two concepts.

Recognized "abnormally dangerous" or "ultra-hazardous" activities are mining, operating rock quarries, rifle ranges, high-voltage electrical stations, hydro-electric dams, nuclear power-plants, crop-dusting, blasting, large building demolition, public fireworks displays, toxic chemical manufacturing/use/storage, and rare/deadly disease laboratories.

A distinguishing characteristic of activities of this type is that they are typically subject to strict safety requirements by government agencies.

Common activities like farming, mowing the lawn, playing with ordinary fireworks, shooting firearms or spraying household insecticide are not "abnormally dangerous".

6. Defenses to Strict Liability Causes of Action

Plaintiffs claiming strict liability causes of action must prove their injuries were caused by the inherently dangerous nature of the activities engaged in by the defendant. Therefore, defendants can always claim the **passive defenses** that the plaintiff's injuries were **caused by acts of God or nature**, or that the injury suffered was **caused events unrelated to the inherent dangers** that make the activity a "strict liability" activity.

Contributory negligence is NOT allowed as a defense, but **comparative fault** may be argued as a defense in some jurisdictions. **Assumption of the risks** is an affirmative defense in all jurisdictions.

Chapter 6: Intentional Tort Causes of Action

There are seven torts that are called "**intentional torts**" because for each of these seven tort causes of action **the plaintiff must prove the defendant acted intentionally**. This is a threshold issue. If the plaintiff cannot prove the defendant acted intentionally, the plaintiff loses. Other torts may be committed deliberately by tortfeasors, but they are not called "intentional torts" because the plaintiff **has no burden to prove** the act was done intentionally.

As with all tort causes of action, plaintiffs claiming intentional tort causes of action must always prove they deserve a remedy, either to compensate them for **damages** suffered, to prevent the tortfeasor an **unjust enrichment**, or to **punish** the tortfeasor. That was explained in Chapter 3.

1. Intentional Acts

An intentional act is one done deliberately to cause a tortuous result, and for each of the intentional torts that necessary "tortuous result" varies. That will be explained below.

An intentional act does not have to be done maliciously, with evil intent, or to deliberately cause any injury at all. It just has to be done to deliberately cause a tortuous result. Often it is an act done in jest and without any intent to cause harm.

> **For example:** Thirsty throws a rotten tomato intending to hit Paul as a joke, and it does hit Paul. It is an intentional tortuous act because he did it to deliberately hit Paul.

An act is also an intentional act if it is deliberately done with knowledge with reasonable certainty it will produce a tortuous result.

> **For example:** Thirsty throws a water balloon off the top of a building into a crowd of people knowing it will almost certainly hit "someone" but without any intent to hit anyone in particular. It is an intentional act.

It is a common mistake of law students to say an "intentional act" is a "volitional act". This is totally wrong. All intentional acts are volitional, but volitional acts are not necessarily intentional acts. A **volitional act** is simply one done voluntarily, on purpose, but it does not have to be done to for the purpose of causing a tortuous result. An intentional act is a **volitional act done for the purpose of causing the tortuous result** that occurs.

> **For example:** Bubba is riding home on a crowded bus, standing in the center aisle. Suddenly the bus lurches. He **volitionally** reaches out and grabs Bambi's ample breast, causing her to be greatly offended. Is it a battery? Only if he reached out **intending to touch her**. But if he reached out intending to grab a support so he would not fall, missed the support and grabbed her breast by accident, it is not an intentional act and not a battery.

If plaintiffs prove defendants intentionally acted to cause a tortuous result, their only other burden is to prove they deserve a remedy because they suffered injury (damages), the tortfeasor reaped an unjust enrichment from the tort (legal restitution), or that the tortfeasor acted with malice, oppression or fraud (exemplary damages).

2. Intentional Failures to Act

If a defendant has a duty to act, and deliberately breaches the duty intending to cause a tortuous result, the defendant is as liable as if they had intentionally acted to cause the same result.

> **For example:** Nurse Ratchet has a duty to provide care to Invalid. When Nurse Ratchet sees invalid about to eat some hot soup, she deliberately does not act thinking it will be funny to see Invalid's reaction to the hot soup. Invalid is burned by the soup. Nurse Ratchet is as liable as she would have been if she deliberately caused Invalid to be burned.

3. Unusually Sensitive Plaintiffs

Plaintiffs who claim a defendant's intentional act injured them must usually prove a "reasonable" person would have been injured by the same act. But sometimes plaintiffs are injured because they are unusually vulnerable to a particular injury that a "reasonable" person would not be injured by. If defendants **act with knowledge** the plaintiffs are peculiarly vulnerable to injury, the plaintiff only has to prove a reasonable person with the same vulnerability would have been injured. These "sensitivities" include peculiar medical conditions and phobias.

> **For Example:** Wheezer is extremely sensitive to cigarette smoke. Winston lights a cigarette in Wheezer's presence, and Wheezer suffers an asthma attack. Generally, Winston will not be liable for battery because an "average person" would not be harmed by "touching" the cigarette smoke. But if Winston acted with knowledge of Wheezer's sensitive condition, he could be liable for battery.

4. The Intentional Torts

There are seven **intentional torts**. They are:

1. **Battery**
2. **Assault**
3. **False Imprisonment**
4. **Trespass to Land**
5. **Trespass to Chattel**
6. **Conversion**
7. **Intentional Infliction of Emotional Distress**

Plaintiffs bringing causes of action for each of these torts must prove the defendant **intentionally acted** (or intentionally failed to act as explained above) and that the act caused either caused them an injury justifying an award of **damages**, that it gave the defendant an unjust enrichment justifying an award of **legal restitution**, or else that the defendant acted with malice, oppression or fraud justifying an award of **exemplary damages**.

--o0o--

A. Battery

To prove a cause of action for **battery** the plaintiff must prove the defendant **intentionally acted to cause** and did cause **a touching of the plaintiff's "person"**. The word "person" means the plaintiff's body, clothing, or some other object in contact with the plaintiff's body or clothing.

In addition, the plaintiff must prove the "touching" caused the plaintiff to suffer **harm** or **reasonable offense**. Offense is "reasonable offense" if the plaintiff claims to have been offended and a "reasonable person" would have been offended in the same circumstance.

> **For example:** Abbie hits Lyndon in the face with a banana crème pie as a political protest stunt, not intending to cause Lyndon any actual injury. Unfortunately Lyndon is allergic to bananas and goes blind. Abbie is liable to Lyndon for battery because he **intended to cause a touching**, did cause a touching, and the touching, in turn, caused Lyndon **injury**.

A tort battery is defined in a very similar manner to a criminal battery. But in tort no "criminal intent" is required. So in tort the plaintiff only has to prove the defendant intended to cause a touching, and that the touching that resulted was harmful or offensive. But the plaintiff does not have to prove the defendant intended for the touching to be harmful or offensive. In criminal law the prosecution must prove the defendant intended to cause a touching with knowledge it would have a harmful or offensive result.

--o0o--

B. Assault

To prove a cause of action for **assault** the plaintiff must prove the defendant **intentionally acted to cause** and did cause the plaintiff **reasonable apprehension of a battery**.

Apprehension of a battery is "reasonable" if a "reasonable person" would have been apprehensive in the same circumstance.

> **For example:** Homer dresses as a scarecrow on Halloween and sits still on his front porch as children approach the door. Suddenly he jumps up and howls to scare the children. Little Lisa is so frightened she goes into hysterics and has to be treated by a child psychologist. Homer is liable, even though he intended no harm.

A tort assault is defined in a very different manner from a criminal assault. In tort no "criminal intent" is required, and the plaintiffs must prove the defendants caused them apprehension of a battery. In criminal law the prosecution must prove the defendant intended to cause EITHER a battery OR apprehension of a battery, and there is no need to prove that any apprehension actually resulted.

--o0o--

C. False Imprisonment

To prove causes of action for **false imprisonment** plaintiffs must prove defendants **intentionally acted** to confine them and did **confine them to a defined area against their will**.

Plaintiffs are **confined** if they have **no reasonable means of escape** that is **reasonably apparent**. And they are **confined against their will** if they **are aware** they are being confined.

A means of escape is **not reasonable if it would expose the plaintiff** to risk of a battery or public ridicule. And a means of escape is not reasonably apparent if it is unlikely a reasonable person with the plaintiff's abilities would have discovered it.

> **For example:** Paul, a blind man, is walking down the sidewalk when Dan warns him to stop and not move because has walked into a nest of deadly snakes. Paul is afraid to move because he is afraid he will be bitten. Actually there are no poisonous snakes at all. Dan is just making fun of Paul's blindness. Dan is liable for false imprisonment because he has intentionally confined Paul to the place where he is standing. It does not matter that there are no "walls" or that a sighted person would have just walked away, as long as a "reasonable blind person" would have been "confined" in the same manner. Dan is also liable for assault. Do you see why?

Plaintiffs claiming false imprisonment must prove they **were aware** of their confinement.

> **For example:** Thirsty falls asleep in a bar. The bartender locks him inside at closing time, and he does not wake up until the janitor comes in the morning. He has no case because he was not aware he was ever confined, and by the time he found out he had been confined he was not confined anymore.

False imprisonment of children is a special case.

> **For example:** Mommy and Brutus have a bitter divorce. The Court awards them joint custody. Mommy takes their child, Sonny, to stay with her parents in Texas who hide him from Brutus. Sonny is happy with that because he doesn't like Brutus either. When Brutus finds Sonny he sues Mommy and her parents, on behalf of Sonny, for false imprisonment. They are all liable to Sonny for false imprisonment because they intentionally confined him (in Texas), and he was aware of that. The fact he was happy and consented to be there is irrelevant because a minor cannot give legal consent to being illegally hidden in violation of a court order.

Never call false imprisonment "false arrest". Never even say "false arrest". It is a forbidden term in law school because there is no such tort.

--o0o--

D. Trespass to Land

To prove causes of action for **trespass to land** plaintiffs must prove defendants **intentionally entered** onto, above, or under their land. Plaintiffs claiming trespass to land always claim the defendants entered their land without permission, but that is a matter of pleading more than an element to be proven.

An intentional entry onto land is any **volitional** or "voluntary" entry, even if the defendant is lost, thinks he has permission to enter, thinks he owns the land he enters, or otherwise makes some "mistake".

> **For example:** Hunter gets lost in the woods and wanders onto Farmer's land thinking that he is still in the National Forest. No matter how "reasonable" his mistake may be, it is an intentional entry because Hunter deliberately went onto the land. And it is Farmer's land.

But an accidental entry onto land is not an intentional entry when it is not voluntary.

> **For example:** Driver hits an icy patch on the road, spins out of control and ends up on Farmer's land. That is not an intentional entry because Driver did not deliberately guide his car onto Farmer's land. His entry is not "volitional" because it was involuntary.

To claim trespass to land for an **entry above** land, the defendant must cause something to cross over the land at an unreasonably low altitude. If aircraft fly over land at normal altitude it is not a trespass to land.

If people, objects, dust, dirt or "particulate matter" are caused to go onto the land, it is a trespass. And if they are left on the land of the plaintiff it is a **continuing trespass**.

But there is no trespass by causing **energy** such as light, heat, noise, radiation or vibration to enter the land. And there is no trespass by causing **smells** to enter the land. However, these acts may give rise to other torts, negligence and nuisance. Negligence and nuisance will be discussed later.

The diversion of **surface water** (rainwater, flood waters, etc.) onto the land of another is generally held to NOT be a trespass to land under the **Common Enemy Doctrine**. That subject is covered more in the study of Real Property.

> **For Example:** Owen aims the downspout on his building to shoot rain water onto Nellie's land. Generally, that is NOT a trespass to land. Owen is only liable if Nellie proves he acted unreasonably.

To drill a well or dig a mine **under** the land of another is a trespass.

A defendant that trespasses onto the land of a plaintiff is liable for all damages caused, and if no other damages are proven the plaintiff still has a legal right to an award of **nominal damages** because the tortfeasor has denied the plaintiff **exclusive possession**, a right of the landowner.

If a trespass to land causes damage that cannot be repaired, damages are generally limited to the market value of the land prior to the trespass. If the damage can be repaired, actual damages have still been limited by some Courts to no more than the market value of the land before the trespass.

Other Courts have held that because land is unique, the market value of the land should not be an absolute limit on the damages awarded.

> **For Example:** Waste from MegaCorp contaminates Owen' home. All Courts hold that Owen has a right to **damages** in the amount of the estimated clean-up costs if they are no more than the market value of his home. But some cases have held that Owen cannot recover more than the market value of the home before the trespass, because that is all he could lose. Other cases suggest that Owen has a right to an award of the actual clean-up costs, even if they exceed the value of his home.

In some cases the plaintiff has a right to a money judgment in legal restitution to prevent the defendant from reaping an unjust enrichment instead of an award of damages.

> **For Example:** Breaker trespasses into Pete's mountain cabin and stays for a week but does not cause any damages. In fact, he leaves the cabin in better condition than it was when he entered. Pete can prove no damages. But Pete has a right to **legal restitution** in the amount it would have cost Breaker to rent a similar cabin for the same period. Otherwise Breaker gains an unjust enrichment from his trespass.

--o0o--

E. Trespass to Chattel

To prove causes of action for **trespass to chattel** plaintiffs must prove defendants **intentionally interfered** with their chattel. This means taking, using, or damaging the personal property of the plaintiff. When a plaintiff seeks an award of **damages** for trespass to chattel, the damages are based on the amount of damage done to the chattel, the plaintiff's loss of use, or repair costs to repair damage done. But the plaintiff may also seek an award of **legal restitution** as an alternative.

> **For example:** Joy takes Beth's car without her permission, drives 1,000 miles, dents the fender and then returns the car. Suppose the wear and tear Joy caused and the cost to repair the fender add up to $500. And suppose Joy would have had to pay $600 to drive a rental car the same distance. Joy intentionally interfered with Beth's chattel, so Beth can bring an action for **trespass to chattel** and obtain a money judgment. Her **damages** are $500, but the unjust enrichment enjoyed by Joy is $600. So to prevent **unjust enrichment** Beth has a right to be awarded $600 rather than her actual "damages" of $500.

Interference with chattel does not have to be done with knowledge that it is the chattel of the plaintiff and can be the result of an "honest mistake".

> **For Example:** Tom accidentally takes Dick's car because both of their cars look alike. Tom is liable for trespass to chattels because he deliberately took the car that he took. If Dick can not prove he suffered any damages, he still has a right to receive **legal restitution** in the amount Tom would have to have paid for a rental car.

Generally, money judgments awarded for trespass to chattel are limited to the market value of the chattel, and if claims exceed the market value of the chattel the claim should more properly be for conversion.

For Example: Tom takes Dick's car and causes damages that will cost $10,000 to repair. The car is only worth $3,000. Dick's claim is generally limited to $3,000 because that is all he actually could lose.

Typically plaintiffs bring an action for trespass to chattel, rather than conversion, when the "interference" is less severe, and they wish to keep their chattel rather than convey it to the tortfeasor, because **the remedy for conversion is a forced sale** of the chattel in dispute to the tortfeasor.

--o0o--

F. Conversion

To prove causes of action for **conversion** plaintiffs must prove exactly the same thing as for trespass to chattel – that the defendants **intentionally interfered** with their chattel. However, **the remedy for conversion is often forced sale of the chattel** to the tortfeasor.

Conversion is always the tort claimed when the tortfeasor has **spent the plaintiff's money**, **destroyed his property** or **substantially deprived the plaintiff of use** of the chattel to the point the plaintiff does not the chattel back.

For example: Joy takes Beth's car without her permission. Beth believes it has been stolen and buys a new car. Beth eventually returns the car. Since Beth was substantially deprived of use, has bought a new car, and does not want her car back, she can bring an action for **conversion** and force Joy to buy the car from her.

Plaintiffs claiming conversion **must prove the defendants have substantially denied them the chattel** involved. If the chattel is only interfered with in a minor way a claim for conversion will be denied, and the proper claim would be trespass to chattel.

A defendant is liable for either conversion or trespass to chattel if they intentionally interfere with the chattel of the plaintiff, but **the defendant does not have to know that the chattel being interfered with belongs to the plaintiff**. If defendant think they are interfering with their own chattel, or that they had permission to use the chattel, they are still liable, no matter how "reasonable" that mistake was. The rule for trespass to chattel and conversion parallels the rule for trespass to land. If the defendant intended to interfere with chattel that belongs to the plaintiff, then they are liable, even if they reasonably believed they were doing the "right thing".

For example: Dan is sitting a bar drinking a margarita and telling everyone he is a law student. He picks up his drink, drains it, and then the person next to him at the bar says, "Hey, dude. You just drank my margarita!" Dan is liable for conversion. It doesn't matter that he reasonably thought the glass he picked up was his own.

It is often said that a person who commits conversion is "strictly liable" meaning that no evidence of malice or wrongful intent needs to be shown. But that is not a good term to use because it has a very different legal meaning. Perhaps a better term would be "strictly responsible".

People who are <u>entrusted with the belongings of others</u> (bailees) are strictly responsible to be sure the goods are not released to anyone but the proper owner.

> **For example:** Bunny stores her furniture at National Storage. Diana goes to National Storage, falsely says that Bunny asked her to get her things, and she is allowed to take Bunny's belongings. National Storage is liable for conversion, no matter how "reasonable" their actions, because they intentionally let Barbara take Bunny's belongings.

But people who are entrusted with the belongings of others are not liable for conversion if the goods are lost because of an accidental event.

> **For example:** Bunny stores her furniture at National Storage. A wildfire burns down the storage facility. National Storage is not liable for conversion because it did not intentionally interfere with her chattel.

While it is common to say the remedy for conversion is a "forced sale" that really means that if the chattel interfered with still exists the Court will tell the tortfeasor to either buy it from the plaintiff and receive title OR the Court will award the plaintiff a money judgment in the same amount, and generally the Court will threaten or order the tortfeasor to return the chattel anyway. So if tortfeasors pay for the chattel they can keep it and if they do not it will be taken from them and they have a judgment awarded against them for the same amount.

If tortfeasors do not buy the chattel in dispute the plaintiffs will still have the same burdens of collecting on the judgment. The Court will not actually "force" the tortfeasor to pay anything.

When an action is brought for conversion of money or something that has been destroyed there is no "forced sale" at all. The remedy is just a money judgment for the amount that was stolen, if the plaintiff seeks **damages**. But the plaintiff can demand award of a larger amount in **legal restitution** if the tortfeasor used the stolen money or property to reap an **unjust enrichment** greater than the actual damages.

Plaintiffs bring an action for trespass to chattel rather than conversion if they want their property back rather than just receive a solely monetary remedy.

> **For Example:** Vick steals Timmy's dog, Lassie. The dog is only worth $100. If Timmy brings an action for **conversion** Vick will be told to buy the dog, and Timmy will lose the dog. But Timmy wants his dog back. So Timmy will bring an action for **trespass to chattel** instead of for conversion, and then seek an **equitable order** to return his dog in **equitable restitution**.

--o0o--

G. Intentional Infliction of Emotional Distress

To prove a cause of action for **intentional infliction of emotional distress** (IIED) the plaintiff must prove the defendant **intentionally committed an outrageous act** which, in turn, caused the plaintiff **extreme emotional distress**.

An act is **outrageous** if reasonable people would view it as a **highly inappropriate, socially unacceptable**, and/or **extremely vulgar** act within the context in which it was committed. An act may not be outrageous in one context while it would be outrageous in an entirely different context.

Any act done for the purpose of causing injury is outrageous per se, but an act may be outrageous even if it was not done for the purpose of causing injury.

Plaintiffs claiming causes of action for IIED must prove the "outrageous act" of the defendant caused them **extreme emotional distress** as evidenced by **hysteria, neurosis, withdrawal, paranoia, revulsion, nausea, insomnia,** or some other evidence of more than mere embarrassment.

If plaintiffs can present evidence of some **physical manifestation** to prove they suffered extreme emotional distress, that would be sufficient. But it is not strictly necessary. Simple testimony describing the extreme emotional distress suffered is sufficient.

> **For example:** Andrew Zimmern eats a live termite in the Amazon jungle for his TV show "Bizarre Foods". Priscilla Prude sees the episode on TV and is extremely distressed. She sues Zimmern for IIED. She will lose because his "act" is not "outrageous". If people in the Amazon jungle eat termites, then it is a socially acceptable practice. And it is not "outrageous" to show that on a TV show dedicated to "Bizarre" eating practices even if the same act would have been "outrageous" where Prude lives.

The only broadly adopted situation in which a plaintiff does not have to present evidence to prove an outrageous act caused extreme emotional distress is something of a fact-bound scenario arising in the 1800s. Railroads treated some corpses in an outrageous manner, and Courts at that time held that if a body of a deceased person is mistreated the close family members can sue for IIED without providing any additional evidence it caused them to be extremely upset. In all other cases such evidence is required.

A claim of IIED is a last resort when no other tort claim can be proven. If the defendant commits ANY other tort the defendant is liable for ALL emotional distress it causes, even very mild distress and IIED does not have to be proven.

> **For example:** Danny breaks into Paul's house (trespass to land), ties him up (false imprisonment), threatens to kill him (assault), hits him on the head (battery), vandalizes his car (trespass to chattel), steals his dog (conversion), makes a lot of noise (nuisance), slanders Paul's reputation (defamation) and crashes into Paul's car (negligence). Danny is liable for all distress Paul suffers, whether it is "extreme" distress or just minor inconvenience, under the other causes of action, and does not have to claim IIED.

5. Transferred Intent

The basic rules of **causation** were explained in Chapter 1, but there is a special causation rule for intentional torts called the **Doctrine of Transferred Intent**. Under the **Doctrine of Transferred Intent** a defendant that **intentionally acts** to cause any tortuous result to anybody is often held liable for every tortuous result caused to everybody, even if the person affected or the result that occurs is not what the defendant originally intended.

> **For Example:** Tom throws a ball intending to frighten Dick, misses and hits Harry. Since Tom intended to cause Dick apprehension of a battery, he intended to assault Dick. But

instead he hit Harry, and he will be liable for a battery to Harry, even though that is not the result that he intended.

Some Courts will not support a claim of transferred intent and will require the plaintiff to prove negligence instead IF the defendant acted **without malice**. Further, Courts generally will NOT allow IIED to be proven by transferred intent.

For Example: Bevis and Butthead frequently pull outrageous stunts on each other. Bevis tips over the church outhouse [3] thinking Butthead is inside. But instead Lady Snob, a social matron, is inside. She is so shocked she takes to her bed. Most Courts would require her to prove Bevis was negligent and will not allow her to claim transferred intent supporting a claim of IIED because he acted without malice. Further, his act was not inherently "outrageous" as it targeted Butthead who had impliedly consented to such acts.

Transferred intent is strictly a tort concept; do not try applying it to criminal law. Crimes are offenses against Society, so if Oswald tries to shoot Kennedy and hits Connolly instead, it is still criminal battery because it was an offense against Society. But if Connolly sues Oswald for tortuous battery he has to prove Oswald intended to cause HIM to be "touched". That is where transferred intent applies. Oswald's intent to hit Kennedy **transfers** into an intent to hit Connolly.

6. Defenses to Intentional Tort Causes of Action

At every stage of every legal action the moving party (movant) has the burden of proving certain legal elements. The initial movant in a tort case is the plaintiff. The other party (respondent) raises defenses in response. The initial respondent in a tort case is the defendant.

There are two types of defenses that may be raised by a respondent in opposition to the movant's case. They are called **passive defenses** and **affirmative defenses**.

Passive defenses are **arguments** by respondents that the movants **have not met their burden** to prove one or more required legal elements of their claim. In the initial stage of tort litigation the plaintiff's **cause of action** is a tort claim, and the defendant raises passive defenses that the plaintiff cannot prove the required legal elements of that cause of action.

An **affirmative defense** is a claim by a respondent that even if a movant can prove every required legal element, **the respondents had a legal right to act** as they did anyway. A tort defendant cannot raise affirmative defenses until after the plaintiff has "rested his case". At that point the defendant becomes the "movant" and the plaintiff becomes the "respondent". If the defendant claims to have an affirmative defense, the **burden shifts to them to prove** each required legal element of claimed affirmative defenses.

For Example: Tom throws a ball and hits Harry. Harry sues Tom for **battery**. Harry is the plaintiff and initial movant. He has the burden of proving each required legal element of his **cause of action**. He must prove Tom intentionally acted to hit him and that it caused him damages. Tom is the defendant and initial respondent. If Tom presents evidence or argument that Harry cannot prove he acted intentionally, or that Harry cannot prove he was

[3] A rustic outdoor toilet.

injured, those are **passive defenses**. When Harry rests his case, Tom has an opportunity to present his defense, and he may claim an **affirmative defense** like **self defense**. Tom becomes the movant, the burden of proof shifts to Tom, and Harry becomes the respondent. Tom must prove the required legal elements of his affirmative defense, that he acted with reasonable force to protect himself. If Harry presents evidence Tom did not use reasonable force it is a **passive defense** against Tom's **affirmative defense** claim he was justified to act as he did.

The affirmative defenses to intentional tort causes of action are in many ways the same as the affirmative defenses to criminal charges. However there is one difference. There is **no affirmative defense of infancy** in tort law. Under the common law there was a conclusive presumption that small children cannot form criminal intent, but this is not an affirmative defense in tort law.

A plaintiff suing a child for a tort must still prove the child intentionally acted to cause the tortuous result, so any defense argument that the child was "too little to know" is always a **passive defense** in a tort case.

The **affirmative defenses** to intentional torts may be remembered by the mnemonic **DARN COPS**:

1. **Discipline**
2. **Authority of Law**
3. **Recapture of Property**
4. **Necessity**
5. **Consent**
6. **Defense of Others**
7. **Defense of Property**
8. **Self Defense**

All of these defenses require the defendant to use only "**reasonable force.**" That means that the defense cannot be claimed unless the defendant only uses the amount of force **necessary**. And **no deadly force** can ever be used to protect or recover **property**. **Deadly force** can ONLY be used when it is **necessary** to protect **people**.

--o0o--

A. Discipline

Defendants may be **privileged to use reasonable force** because of their **position of authority**. This is usually a defense to an action for **false imprisonment** and **battery**. The defendant must show that their actions were **necessary, justified** and **reasonable**. This is a rare defense for those people who have a need to enforce discipline and order (e.g. **teachers, bus drivers, pilots, ship captains, etc.**) It is not discussed by some texts, and it overlaps the defense of **necessity.**

> **For Example:** Ms. Ballbreaker the gym teacher detains Porky in her office and raps his knuckles with a ruler for misbehaving. She is not liable for false imprisonment and battery if her action was within the school rules authorizing corporal punishment and reasonably necessary to maintain school decorum.

--o0o--

B. Authority of Law

Defendants may be **privileged by authority of law** to use **reasonable force** to **arrest or detain** the plaintiff. It is usually a defense to a claim of **false imprisonment** or **battery**. This may also be called **crime prevention**. The law disfavors private parties (not police) from "playing cop" unless the facts clearly warrant it.

1) Arrest with warrant

This applies only to police. Tort law favors arrest under authority of a warrant. Any arrest **with a warrant** is privileged if 1) the **person named** on the warrant is arrested, 2) the warrant **appears valid** and 3) **no unreasonable force** is used. Honest mistakes are generally defensible.

2) Arrest without warrant

Tort law disfavors an arrest without a warrant unless it actually prevents a crime.

3) Crime prevention

The law favors crime prevention. Any arrest **without a warrant to prevent crime** is privileged if it is 1) to **prevent** 2) an **apparent felony, breach of the peace**, or misdemeanor threatening **significant harm** (more than minor harm) to people or property 3) **presently being or about to be committed** and 4) **reasonable force** is used. Mistakes are allowed. This situation is often recognized as a separate and distinct tort defense. This defense essentially overlaps the defenses of public or private **necessity, self defense, defense of others** and **defense of property.**

> **For Example:** Tom goes into Dick's jewelry shop. Harry mistakenly believes he saw Tom hide some valuable jewelry inside his jacket. As Tom begins to hurriedly leave the store Harry takes his arm and stops him. Although Harry is wrong, and Tom has taken nothing, Harry is not liable for **assault** or **battery** because he acted **reasonably** to **prevent a crime** that **appeared to be committed in his presence**. However, Harry's action would not be defensible if he used unreasonable force.

4) Arrest for past felonies

- **Police** may arrest for **past felonies without a warrant** on a 1) **reasonable belief** that a **felony occurred** and 2) the **plaintiff is the guilty party**. Mistakes are allowed.

- **Private parties** (not police) can only arrest **for past felonies without a warrant** only if 1) it is **known for a fact** that a felony occurred and 2) there is **reasonable belief the plaintiff is guilty**. Mistakes are only allowed if there was, in fact, a felony.

5) Arrest for misdemeanors in fresh pursuit

Any arrest **without a warrant** is privileged if 1) the **defendant witnesses** a **breach of peace** (act of violence or disruption) committed **by the plaintiff,** 2) the defendant is in **fresh pursuit** of the plaintiff and 3) **reasonable force** is used. NO MISTAKES ARE ALLOWED!

For Example: Dick vandalizes Paul's car and runs away. Paul chases Dick but gets confused and tackles Vic, an innocent bystander. Paul is liable to Harry for **battery** because he MADE A MISTAKE. Sorry, Paul. But if Paul had caught Dick he would be privileged to arrest him for vandalism.

--o0o--

C. Recapture of Property

Defendants may be **privileged to recover (recapture) their own land and personal property** in certain circumstances. This may be a defense to actions for **trespass to land, trespass to chattels, false imprisonment, assault** and **battery**.

A "recapture of property" is distinguished from a "defense of property" because the property of the defendant has already been lost, and the defendant is acting to recover it. Generally, there are three common situations when there is a **right of recapture**.

1) Re-entry to land

A defendant may be privileged to enter onto and retake possession of land claimed by the plaintiff. The right to recapture land is often controlled by statutes, and the law varies substantially among States. But as far as common law is concerned the following is generally true.

- RECENT WRONGFUL POSSESSION. A defendant is **privileged** to use **reasonable force** (not deadly force!) to remove a trespasser and the trespasser's belongings from the defendant's land if the plaintiff **recently entered** the land with **no legal right to occupy** the land. This is almost the same thing as **defense of property** and a defense to **assault, battery, trespass to land** and **trespass to chattels.**

  For Example: Homeless Harry enters Owen's land without permission dragging a shopping cart full of junk. He falsely claims he has a right to live there. It Owen quickly uses reasonable force to remove Harry and his shopping cart from his land he will not be liable for **assault, battery, trespass to land** or **trespass to chattels** because Harry's occupation of the land is 1) **recent** and 2) **wrongful from the beginning**.

- PEACEFUL RETAKING. A defendant is **privileged** to **peacefully take possession of property** from one who EITHER **never had any right to possess the property** or else whose **right of possession has terminated. No force or threat of force** may be used **against a tenant or the tenant's possessions**.

  For Example: Tom loans his car to Dick. Dick refuses to return the car falsely claiming that Tom gave it to him as a gift. If Tom finds the car parked somewhere and can retake possession peacefully, he is privileged to retake possession of his car in virtually all jurisdictions. If Dick has left possessions in the car Tom must keep them safe.

The right to recapture land from a "holdover" tenant or long-term trespasser is similar but more likely to be strictly limited by statute.

For Example: Tom leases land to Dick. At the end of the lease Dick refuses to vacate. In Dick's absence Tom is often privileged to enter and take control of the land (changing the locks, etc.) as long as he does not use force against Dick and does not disturb or damage Dick's possessions. However many modern jurisdictions strictly prohibit this and require the landlord to follow statutory eviction procedures.

2) Recapture of chattels

A defendant may be privileged to **reasonably enter** the land (but not the dwelling) of another and otherwise use **reasonable force** or threat of force to **retake** possession of chattel that has been **wrongfully taken** from the defendant. This is a defense to claims of **trespass to land, assault** and **battery**. It is also very similar in scope to **defense of property** and **private necessity.**

- WRONGFUL TAKING. The **wrongful taking** can be by **any means beyond the control of the defendant** including **theft**, **force**, **fraud**, or **acts of God or nature** but NOT willful acts or negligence of the defendant.

- ENTRY TO LAND. The **reasonable entry** of land to recapture chattel must be at a **reasonable time and manner** including **first requesting return** of the chattel if that is a practical act. It is NOT reasonable to forcibly enter the dwelling of another to recapture chattel. **Fresh pursuit is not necessary** to justify the defendant's entry of land to recapture chattel. But the defendant will be liable for any damage to the plaintiff's property when the plaintiff did not wrongfully take the defendant's chattel.

- FORCE AGAINST THE PERSON. The use of **reasonable force** to retake chattel away from the plaintiff requires that the wrongful taking be **recent** so that the defendant is in **fresh pursuit** of the chattel.

For Example: Tom's cows wander away after a storm blows down his fence. Tom finds one cow in Dick's pasture. Dick is not there, so Tom cuts Dick's fence and leads the cow home. Tom is NOT liable for **trespass** to Dick's land, BUT he **has to repair Dick's fence** because it was **not Dick's fault** the cow got out. Then Tom sees Harry taking another cow. Tom demands possession but Harry refuses. Tom moves forward and threatens the use of reasonable force to take the cow. Tom is NOT liable for assault because he was in **fresh pursuit** and used **reasonable force** to recapture his **wrongfully taken** cow.

--o0o--

D. Necessity

A defendant has a **privilege to use reasonable force to protect people or property** in an **emergency**. It is a defense to **all intentional torts**. This defense overlaps several other defenses including **recapture of property, defense of property, self-defense,** and **defense of others**.

Criminal law is more apt to call this **defense of property, self-defense,** and/or **defense of others**. Tort law is more apt to call it **necessity**, especially when the facts suggest **public necessity**.

As with all affirmative defenses, necessity allows only **reasonable** force. The use of force is not reasonable if it is not necessary, and there is NO privilege to inflict great bodily injury on an innocent party. Further, the use of force to protect property is **not reasonable if it causes more damage than it prevents**.

> **For Example:** Tom pushes bystander Dick out of the way to save victim Harry from a burning building. Tom has no right to use deadly force. But if Dick tried to prevent the rescue Tom could use deadly force in **defense** of Harry. In that case the defense would be more akin to "defense of others".

1) Public necessity

Defendants have an **absolute privilege** to use reasonable force to protect the **property of others, even if they are also protecting their own property as well.** In this case the defendant is not liable for ANY property damage that results because it is considered a **public necessity**.

If an employee within the **scope of employment** acts to only protect property of the employer, the "property of others" is not being protected, and the act is not one of public necessity. But if the employee is acting to protect the property of other parties besides the employer it is an act of public necessity.

2) Private necessity

Defendants have a **qualified privilege** to use reasonable force to protect only **their own property**. In this case the defendant IS liable for property damage that results because it is a **private necessity**.

> **For Example:** Tom's house is on fire. He breaks into Dick's hardware store to get a fire extinguisher to put out the fire. He is liable to Dick for ANY of the damages he caused if his act did not protect anyone's property but his own. He then must reimburse Dick for the damages he caused during the break-in.

--o0o--

E. Consent

A claim of **consent** is a claim the defendant was **privileged** to act because the **plaintiff consented** to the act. It is a defense to **all intentional torts**. Consent is perhaps the most common and important of all tort defenses because the plaintiff cannot complain of the defendant's act if the plaintiff **effectively approved** of the defendant's act.

> **For Example:** Bevis goes out for the school football team. Butthead tackles Bevis and breaks his arm. Butthead is not liable for **battery** because Bevis **impliedly consented** to be tackled (a harmful or offensive touching) when he asked to join the football team.

1) Consent by minors and incompetents

Minors and **incompetents** cannot give effective consent to acts that pose **risks they cannot appreciate** because of their incapacity. But consent may be given for a person lacking capacity by a guardian.

For Example: Sixteen-year-old Bambi agrees to let Bevis tattoo the name of her boyfriend, Butthead, on her breast. Bevis is liable for **battery** because Bambi is a minor and her express consent is ineffective.

But generally, minors CAN give effective consent to <u>acts of the type the child has regularly been authorized to approve</u>.

For Example: Timmy lives in a house with a large sign on the front gate that says "Keep Out." Homeless Harry asks Timmy, a five-year-old child, if he can enter the yard to drink from the garden hose. Timmy's consent will be effective <u>if he has regularly been allowed to let his playmates and other people enter the yard.</u>

2) Fully informed consent required

Consent is not effective if the plaintiff is **not fully and accurately informed** by the defendant of the risks posed by a proposed act. Where the defendant has information that the plaintiff needs to make an informed decision and the plaintiff is **reasonably unaware** of that information, the defendant has a duty to reveal it to the plaintiff.

For Example: Doctor Butthead prescribes a drug for Bevis without revealing the side effects will render him sterile. Butthead's act of prescribing the drug is **battery** because it is an intentional act to cause a harmful touching. Bevis' following of the doctor's orders is not an effective implied consent because he was **not fully informed.**

3) Consent obtained by misrepresentation

Consent obtained as a result of trick, fraud, misrepresentation or concealment is never legally effective.

For Example: Buffy goes to Doctor Smut for an examination. Bevis attends the examination dressed in a white lab coat and carefully observes. Buffy consents to the "touching" by Doctor Smut in this situation because she reasonably believes Bevis is a medical professional. If she later discovers Bevis is not a medical professional, Doctor Smut is liable for **battery** because it was an <u>offensive touching</u> under these circumstances, and she did not give <u>fully informed consent</u> to be "touched" in this manner.

4) Implied consent

Consent may be **implied** by circumstances or the statements and actions of the plaintiff. Shoppers and patrons have implied consent to enter retail establishments. People have implied consent to approach the front door of a residence. Defendants have implied consent to engage in **socially customary practices** such as shaking hands.

5) Revocation of consent

Consent is effective until it is revoked, and it is no revoked until the defendant receives **actual notice** of the revocation.

> **For Example:** Thirsty is a "regular" patron at Joe's Bar. He has implied consent to enter. One day Joe posts a sign at the door that says "Closed today for private party". Thirsty comes to the bar as usual, does not see the sign, and enters through the front door. As he pushes open the door it knocks over and destroys a TV. Thirsty is not liable for trespass to land because he had implied consent to enter and it was never revoked because he did not see the sign. He may be liable for negligence however.

6) Legally prohibited consent

Consent, either express or implied, is not effective to an **act that is illegal** (except see immediately below) or one that poses **significant likelihood of serious physical injury** to the plaintiff. For example, a plaintiff cannot effectively consent to be killed or mutilated. Statutes often prohibit certain acts to prevent foreseeable harm. Consent to such an illegal act is ineffective as a defense against a claim of the very harm the act was intended to prevent.

7) Consensual illegal fighting

If a plaintiff and defendant agree to engage in an **illegal fight** (e.g. a duel) the general view is that **consent is effective as to each party** because otherwise plaintiffs would benefit from their illegal acts. Under this view defendants who escalate the level of violence cannot claim consent as a defense because the plaintiffs did not consent to the escalated level of violence.

Under an alternate view consent is never an effective defense because there is no legal right to consent to illegal acts.

--o0o--

F. Defense of Others

Defendants are **privileged to use reasonable force to protect others from apparent, immediate and wrongful harm by an aggressor**. In the early common law some Courts held that there was no privilege to protect strangers, and there was only a privilege to protect family members. That idea was abandoned so long ago it is not worth mentioning.

Defense of others is simply a subcategory of the **defense of public necessity**. If it is necessary to protect other people from harm it can either be called public necessity or defense of others.

1) Defense must be reasonably necessary

As with all tort defenses, there is no privilege to use **unreasonable force.** Force is only reasonable if it is **apparently necessary**. Therefore, an **officious intermeddler** has no privilege to get unnecessarily involved in the minor arguments and scuffles of others or to act with unnecessary force.

> **For Example:** Tom, Dick and Harry are in a bar. Tom says, "Dick, I'm going to kick your (*burp!*) ass as soon as I can get to my (*burp!*) feet." Harry jumps up and hits Tom over the head with a pool cue. Harry is liable for **battery** and he cannot claim **defense of others** because his act was not reasonably necessary to protect Dick. He is an "**intermeddler**".

2) No privilege to protect aggressors

The privilege to defend others only applies to defending others from **wrongful harm.** Therefore, there is no privilege of "defense of others" to protect **aggressors** against their victims.

An aggressor is one who **starts** a fracas, **escalates the level of violence** of a fracas, or **continues** a fracas after the other parties seek to withdraw from it.

There is a MAJOR SPLIT in the Courts on whether defendants are privileged to claim **defense of others** when they **accidentally help the aggressor** in a fight. The two views on this called the "Step into the Shoes" view and the "Reasonable Appearances" view.

3) The "step-into-the-shoes" view

Under one view defendants who accidentally aid aggressors **cannot claim defense of others** as a defense at all. Under this view they are said to **step into the shoes** of the aggressor, and since the aggressor in a fight cannot claim self-defense, the defendants cannot claim defense of others.

4) The "reasonable appearances" view

Under a different view defendant who accidentally aid aggressors can claim defense of others but have the burden to prove they acted because the aggressor **reasonably appeared to be the innocent victim** of aggression.

--o0o--

G. Defense of Property

Defendants are **privileged to use reasonable force to protect property from apparent, immediate and wrongful harm by others**.

If the defendant's own property is at risk the defense is essentially the same as "private necessity", and if the property of others is at risk the defense is essentially the same as "public necessity".

1) Reasonable force, not deadly force

Defendants are only **privileged to use reasonable force to defend property** from harm.
The use of "reasonable force" means the defendant is privileged to act and use force based on the **facts as they reasonably appear to be**.

But it is **never reasonable to use deadly force to protect property** (as opposed to protecting people from harm.) And force is only reasonable to the degree it is **necessary**. And, it is not reasonable to **cause more damage protecting property than the property is worth**.

If the defendant uses unreasonable force to protect property, the **privilege is lost** and the **defendant becomes an aggressor**. Further, that may then justify the use of deadly force by the plaintiff against the defendant.

The defendant can use reasonable force to 1) prevent **apparent trespassers from entering or using** property of the defendant, 2) to **eject apparent trespassers** from property of the defendant, 3) to **prevent taking of or damage** to personal property of the defendant, and 4) to **detain and question** those apparently responsible to damage to the defendant's property as well witnesses to the event causing damage for a reasonable time, and in a reasonable manner **to protect litigation rights**.

> **For Example:** Vickie sees her car on fire with Aaron watching it burn. Aaron refuses to answer her questions and starts to leave. Vickie is privileged to forcibly detain Aaron for a reasonable period of time to investigate who he is, who set her car on fire, etc. because it is necessary to protect her litigation rights. Those rights are an intangible form of personal property, and she has the right to act in a reasonable manner to protect that property.

2) Deadly traps strictly prohibited

It is strictly prohibited to use concealed deadly devices like "booby traps" or guns rigged to trip-wires to protect property.

3) No right to cause deadly peril to defend property

Defense of property does not justify **exposing people to deadly perils**.

> **For Example:** Tom stumbles into Dirty Dick's desert camp dying from thirst. Dick refuses to let Tom have any water. Tom pulls a gun demanding water. Dick strikes him to protect his water. Tom kills Dick and drinks his water. **Defense of property** did not justify Dick in denying Tom water because that exposed him to possible death from thirst. By denying Tom access to the water Dick became the **aggressor**. That gave Tom the right to use reasonable force to protect himself in **self-defense**.

4) Shopkeeper's privilege

Business proprietors have the right to use **reasonable force** to detain a person **reasonably suspected** of stealing merchandise or sneaking onto the premises without paying an entry fee for a **reasonable period** to investigate and summon police. [4] This is simply a particular application of the **defense of property** privilege.

> **For Example:** Bevis, a movie theater employee, suspects that Butthead has entered the theater without paying for a ticket. He leads Butthead to the manager's office and questions him for four hours before letting him leave. Bevis is liable for false imprisonment because **four hours is an unreasonable period** of time to hold Butthead.

5) Prevention of trespass to land or chattel

A person is privileged to use reasonable force to prevent trespass to their land or chattel. This is so obvious it goes unsaid, and because it is unsaid law students seem to lose sight of the obvious.

---

[4] This is a good example of how virtually every aspect of the law hinges on reasonable behavior. With the rare exception of "strict liability" offenses, a person who acts reasonably is seldom going to be liable.

> **For Example:** Thirsty gets drunk and Joe's Bar and is told to leave. That revokes his implied consent to be there. Thirsty refuses to leave. That makes him a trespasser. Joe has a right to use reasonable force to protect his property (the Bar). He grabs Thirsty and tosses him out the door. He is privileged to do that unless he uses unreasonable force.

--oOo--

H. Self-Defense

Defendants are **privileged to use reasonable force to protect themselves from harm by an aggressor**. The use of force against a person is only reasonable if it is **apparently necessary to defend the victim of an attack by an aggressor**, a person who **started** a fracas, **escalated the level of violence**, or **acted to continue** the fracas after other parties sought to withdraw.

1) No duty to retreat

Under the MAJORITY view the defendant **never has a duty to retreat** from an altercation. But under a MINORITY view the defendant is only privileged to use **deadly force** if there is **no reasonable means of retreat** from the altercation with the aggressor. Modernly all Courts agree there is **no duty to retreat within the defendant's home.**

2) Identifying the aggressor

The defendant is NOT privileged to claim self-defense if they are the **aggressor** in the altercation **at the time of the tortuous act.**

The **initial aggressor** in a fracas (altercation, fight, violent confrontation) is the person who **starts** it, and the other party is the **victim**. But if a victim **unreasonably escalates the level of violence** the victim becomes the aggressor, and the aggressor becomes the victim. If an aggressor **attempts to withdraw** from the fracas and the victim acts to continue the violence, the aggressor becomes the victim, and the victim becomes the aggressor.

> **For Example:** Bernie is confronted by hoodlums on the subway. They threaten him with a screwdriver and demand money. They are the aggressors. Bernie pulls a gun and the hoodlums begin to flee. They are no longer aggressors. Bernie chases them, shooting. He is the aggressor at the time he shoots. Bernie has no right to claim self-defense.

7. Intentional Torts Distinguished from Negligence

There are **two main reasons** a tort plaintiff would rather prove the defendant committed an intentional tort rather than negligence.

First, if a plaintiff can prove a tort was intentional and also prove the defendant acted with malice, oppression or fraud, the plaintiff can seek an award of **punitives**. But there are no punitive awards for negligence.

Second, if a plaintiff can prove a tort was intentional the defendant cannot raise the defenses of **contributory negligence** (or **comparative negligence**) and **assumption of the risk**. This is a major difference.

Chapter 7: Negligence

In plain English "negligence" means the **failure to exercise the degree of care that a reasonable person would use** in the same situation.[5] But to prevail in a Court of law plaintiffs claiming negligence must prove two additional facts. They must prove the defendants **had a duty** to act as a reasonable person would and that the failure of the defendant to act in a reasonable manner **caused the plaintiff damages**.[6]

Punitives are **never awarded for negligent acts**, unless there is proof of **gross negligence** or **recklessness** as those terms were defined in Chapter 3.

As explained earlier, it is an **intentional tort** for a defendant to **breach a duty to act** deliberately intending to cause a tortuous result. In contrast, NEGLIGENCE is a **breach of a duty to act** out of carelessness, accident or inadvertence and NOT for the purpose of causing a tortuous result.

The plaintiff seeking an award of damages for negligence must prove **five legal elements**:

- That the defendant **had a duty** to act as a reasonable person would act;
- That the defendant **breached** his duty to act in a reasonable manner;
- That the defendant's breach was the **actual cause** of the plaintiff's injury;
- That the defendant's breach was the **proximate cause** of the plaintiff's injury; and
- The **damages** caused by the defendant's breach.[7]

1. No General Duty to Act!

The **general rule** is that people have NO DUTY to act in any way to help or protect others from harm. **This is very important**. It is often misunderstood, and it cannot be overemphasized.

> **For Example:** Han sees Princess Leah being seized by Imperial storm troopers and does nothing to help her. He is certainly "negligent" in the plain English meaning of that word because a "reasonable person" would do something to help her. But Han is not **legally liable** unless he **has a duty to act** and his failure to act **causes her damages**.

In your studies you may read statements such as, "Everyone has a general duty to act reasonably to prevent harm to others." Statements such as this are TOTAL HOGWASH and reveal a deep and serious lack of understanding of the law.

[5] I like plain English, it's my mother tongue.

[6] I have been unable to conceive of any possible scenario in which negligence would cause the tortfeasor to reap an unjust enrichment.

[7] As explained below, this is not exactly correct but it is usually correct.

2. Creation of a Duty to Act

But while there is no "general duty", there are **five conditions** that do **create a duty** **to act**. They can be remembered by the mnemonic **SCRAP**:

- **Statutory** duties: A duty to act can always be **created by a statute**;
- **Contractual** duties: A duty to act can always be **created by a contract**;
- **Relationship** duties: People in particular **relationships** have duties by common law;
- **Assumption** of a duty: People can **voluntarily assume** duties; and
- **Peril** duties: People who create **reasonably foreseeable peril** to others have a duty.

When a defendant owes a plaintiff a duty, it is called a **duty of due care**. The exact meaning of that varies, but in almost every case it means a duty to **act as reasonably necessary** to protect others from harm.

--o0o--

A. Duties Created by Statute; Negligence per Se

A statute can create a duty. Typical statutes of this type are the duty of doctors and emergency personnel to rescue and treat ill patients, the duty of motorists to stop and give assistance at traffic accidents, and the duty of medical workers, social workers and school teachers to report suspected child abuse or abuse of the elderly. [8] Here a "statute" means a law, not some "company rule".

A duty created by a statute is **strictly defined** by the statute. If a defendant **violates a statute**, and the violation **causes injury**, the defendant is said to be **negligent per se** if and only if:

1) The injury caused is the **TYPE the statute was supposed to prevent**, and
2) The plaintiff is in the **CLASS of people the statute was supposed to protect**.

Proof of negligence per se simultaneously establishes both **duty** and **breach** because the statute creates the duty and the violation of the statute proves the breach. Beyond that the plaintiffs must only prove **causation** and **damages** along with the **purpose of the statute.**

> **For Example:** Don fishes from a bridge in violation of a "no fishing" ordinance intended to prevent traffic accidents on the bridge. Paula is swimming in the river below. If Don negligently injures Paula he **is not negligent per se** because the ordinance was not intended to protect "swimmers" in the river below the bridge. So if Paula claims Don was negligent she has to prove he owed her a duty of due care for some other reason.

Negligence per se is **often tested** on examinations but is **seldom a viable claim** by the plaintiff because if the defendant is really negligent per se it makes the exam question far too easy and students will be left with too much time on their hands. So the injury caused will often not be the

---

[8] Many other statutes require people to do certain things in certain circumstances, but it is not clear if they create duties or just define the standard of due care as to duties that already exist. For example drivers may be required to put child passengers in "child safety" seats, but the driver is already placing the child in peril, so a duty to act reasonably to protect the child already exists. The statute is not creating a duty as much as defining the standard of due care the driver is expected to meet.

type the statute was intended to prevent, or the plaintiff is not in the class the statute was intended to protect.

--o0o--

B. Duties Created by Contract

A defendant who enters into a contract has a **contractual duty** to act as promised. If a contract breach only causes monetary losses, the remedies of the non-breaching party are determined by contract law, not tort law. And contract law only provides compensation for monetary losses that are the direct consequence of the breach. That effectively means contract law only compensates for losses that are called "**special damages**" in tort law. Contract law does not provide any compensation for pain, suffering, inconvenience, emotional distress or other injuries that are called "**general damages**" in tort law. [9]

> **For Example:** Paula pays Don to replace the brake pads on her car. Don negligently fails to repair the brakes properly, and Paula has to pay a different mechanic $500 to repair the brakes properly. Don breached his contractual duty to Paula and is liable **in contract law** for her damages in the amount of $500. Don is not liable for any inconvenience or emotional distress his breach causes Paula in contract law.

But if a contract breach causes an "event" producing **personal injury and property damage,** tort law provides a remedy, including compensation for **general damages**. This means such things as pain, suffering, inconvenience, and emotional distress.

> **For Example:** Paula pays Don to replace the brake pads on her car. Don negligently fails to repair the brakes properly, Paula crashes, her car is destroyed, she suffers serious injury, and she is permanently disfigured. Don breached his duty to repair the brakes properly, and he is liable to her **in tort law** for all of her property damage, her lost wages, and her medical expenses. Those are her **special damages**. But tort law also makes Don liable for her pain, suffering, inconvenience, and emotional distress. Those are her **general damages**.

Duties based on contract are **defined by the contract** alone, and do not extend to protect unintended parties.

> **For Example:** Mother hires Sitter to watch her boy, Sonny, while she is at work. Sitter negligently lets Sonny go out the door, and he burns down Neighbor's house. Sitter owed Mother and Sonny a duty of due care, but they were not injured. She did not owe Neighbor a duty of due care because he was not a party to the contract, and he was not an intended third party beneficiary of the contract. Her contract with Mother did not obligate her to protect Neighbor from Sonny. [10]

--o0o--

---

[9] The terms "special" and "general" should be strictly confined to tort law discussion because monetary damages directly resulting from a breach are universally called "special damages". But in contract law some people want to call monetary losses "general damages". That just causes unnecessary confusion.

[10] This is a hard concept for law students. Think about it. Sitter is not getting paid to protect Neighbor from Sonny. So is not liable to Neighbor for what Sonny did. Sonny caused Neighbor's loss, so Sonny is liable to Neighbor, not Sitter. If Neighbor sued Sonny, perhaps Sonny could sue Sitter on a cross-complaint because he would not be liable to Neighbor if Sitter had done her job. But clearly Sitter is not directly liable to Neighbor for any reason.

C. Duties Created by Relationships

Under tort law certain relationships between parties create **duties of due care**. Some of the more common **relationship duties** are:

1. **Spouses** have a duty to protect **each other;**
2. **Parents** have a duty to protect **minor children**;
3. **Ship captains, airplane pilots, etc.** have duties to protect **passengers** and **crew**;
4. **Employers** have a duty to protect **employees**;
5. **Business partners** have a duty to protect **the partnership**;
6. **Corporate promoters, officers** and **directors** have a duty to protect **the corporation**;
7. **Schools** have a duty to protect **students** (more so for minors; less so for adults);
8. **Teachers** have a limited duty to protect **students** (within the classroom);
9. **Doctors** have a duty to protect their patients from disease;
10. **Lawyers** owe a duty to protect their clients from legal liability;
11. **Inn-keepers** have a duty to protect **guests** from harm;
12. **Sellers of land** have a duty to inform **buyers** about known property defects;
13. **Bailees** (people entrusted to hold the property of others) have a duty to protect property of **bailors** (those who entrust property to bailees) from loss or harm;
14. **Trustees** have a duty to protect the **trust** from financial losses;
15. **Executors** (or "personal representatives") have a duty to protect the **estate** from financial losses;
16. **Guardians** have a duty to protect the **ward** from harm;
17. **Conservators** have a duty to protect the **conservatee** from harm;
18. **Occupiers of land** owe certain duties to **people on the land** and to **people off the land.** This is called **premises liability**; and
19. **Landlords** owe certain duties to **tenants** and **others on and off the land** (also **premises liability**).

    For Example: Night clerk Tom rents a room in Seedy Hotel to Dick. In the night Tom hears there is smoke on the third floor. Tom has a duty to alert Dick to the danger because he is an "inn-keeper" and Dick is a "guest".

It is important to keep in mind those who do NOT have **relationship duties**:

1. **Spouses** have NO relationship duty to protect **other people** from their spouse;
2. **Children** have NO relationship duty to **parents** (the opposite of many Asian cultures);
3. **Siblings** have NO relationship duty to **each other**;
4. **Parents** have NO relationship duty to protect **other people** from their children UNLESS they KNOW the child presents a clear danger to others;
5. **Employees** have a contractual duty, but NO relationship duty to **employers**;
6. **Businesses** have NO relationship duty to **customers**;
7. **Students** have NO relationship duty to **schools** or **teachers**;
8. **Patients** have NO relationship duty to **doctors**;
9. **Clients** have NO relationship duty to **lawyers**;
10. **Guests** have NO relationship duty to **inn-keepers, hosts** or to **other guests**;
11. **Tenants** have a duty to **Landlords** but only under real property law, not tort law;
12. **Occupiers of land** have no duty to **unknown trespassers except children**;

13. **Wards** have NO relationship duty to **Guardians**;
14. **Conservatees** have NO relationship duty to **Conservators**;
15. **Estates** have a duty to **Executors** but only by statute, not tort law;
16. **Buyers of land** have NO relationship duty to **sellers**;
17. **Neighbors** have NO relationship duty to **each other**;
18. **Strangers** have NO relationship duty to **each other**;
19. **Policemen**, **firemen**, and other **government employees** have NO relationship duty to the **public**;

    For Example: Tom sees his cousin Dick hanging from a cliff in mortal danger. Tom does nothing to help because he hates Dick. Tom is not liable under the common law because he has no relationship duty to protect his cousin.

1) Family duties

Under common law **spouses** owe a duty to care and protect each other. And parents owe a relationship duty **<u>to their minor children</u>** to care for and protect them. Parents do not owe any duty to adult children.

There are no other relationship duties between family members. In other words, children never owe any relationship duty to parents, siblings do not owe any duty to each other, grandparents own no duties to grandchildren, aunts, uncles, and cousins never owe any duty to anyone else.

Statutes may create some other duty between family members, but there is no relationship duty.

Some Courts have held that parents have a relationship duty to take **warn other people** if they know their children pose **likely harm** to them.

> **For Example:** Mommy lets her 17 year old son, Sonny, go outside. He goes next door and burns down Neighbor's house. Mommy had a duty to <u>care for and protect Sonny</u>. But she had no duty to protect Neighbor from Sonny <u>unless she knew</u> Sonny was **likely** to burn down Neighbor's house, and many Courts don't even recognize a duty in that situation. Neighbor's cause of action is against Sonny, not Mommy.

2) The duties of landlords, occupiers of land, sellers of land

Landlords, **occupiers of land** and **sellers of land** have relationship duties to people who may be injured by activities and conditions on the land. This is called **premises liability**. It is probably the most difficult and important of all relationship duties.

An **occupier of land** may be an owner of the land or a tenant. A **landlord** is one who leases or rents real property to a **tenant**. A tenant may be an occupier of land or may in turn sublease to a sub-tenant, and in that case they become landlords as to the subtenant. If landlords retain control over any part of the land (e.g. hallways, parking lots, courtyards, lobby) they are **occupiers** of that portion of the land, and a **landlord** as to the part they have leased to a tenant.

The duties of landlords, occupiers of land and sellers of land to various potential plaintiffs vary depending on the categorization of the plaintiffs. This is explained in detail separately below.

--o0o--

D. Duties Created by Assumption

A person who **expressly or impliedly assumes a duty** has a duty to act as promised.

> **For Example:** Tom sees Dick drowning. Dick cries out for help, and Tom says, "I will save you." By this statement Tom has **promised** to save Dick. By this act he **assumed a duty** to act reasonably to rescue Dick. If he then fails to make a reasonable effort to rescue Dick, he will be liable for the injuries it causes Dick.

Duties based on assumption are **defined by the express or implied promises** of the defendant, as a reasonable person would believe them to be, and do not extend to parties or duties beyond that.

A duty may be **impliedly assumed** by participating in a **joint activity**. The duty is defined by and limited to the express or implied promise arising from participation.

> **For Example:** Hans and Fritz go backpacking together. Hans breaks his leg. Fritz has a duty to help him. By participating in a joint activity he assumed a duty to take reasonable steps to aid Hans. If he just walks away and abandons Hans. If he does he will be liable for the injuries it causes. [11]

A duty may be impliedly assumed by **accepting employment** or **joining an organization** with stated policies or procedures.

> **For Example:** Pamela joins a youth group that requires members to report child abuse. She has **assumed** a duty. If she learns that another member, Mary, is being abused she has a duty to report it and may be liable if she breaches her duty.

The only substantial difference between a duty created by a contract and a duty created by assumption is that in a contract there is an exchange of consideration. A promise or agreement that is not contractual creates an assumed duty.

--o0o--

E. Duties Created by Peril

A person who does something that creates **reasonably foreseeable dangers** (peril) to other people has a duty to act to protect others from the dangers they have created. [12] This is a **duty created by peril**, and perhaps the most often tested area of negligence.

The creation of peril is not by itself a “negligent” act. In fact, it is impossible to live a normal life without creating some reasonably foreseeable risks others might be hurt. The duty of the defendant is simply to takes reasonable precautions to prevent others from being injured.

---

[11] But if Bevis was not backpacking WITH Butthead and simply found him injured in the forest, Bevis would have no duty to help him at all, absent some statute to the contrary.

[12] The term “reasonably foreseeable” means that a reasonable person in the same circumstance would realize that the act creates a risk that others might be injured.

For Example: Driver drives his car. That act creates reasonably foreseeable peril to others. Driver' duty is to drive carefully. If he does that, he is not negligent.

A corollary to the general rule is that a person who does not create reasonably foreseeable dangers to others has **no duty** to protect anyone from the dangers they have created.

In general modern Courts hold that **people who create reasonably foreseeable peril** to others **are liable to anyone who is a foreseeable plaintiff**. But Courts often disagree who foreseeable plaintiffs are.

1) The Rescuer Doctrine

Under the RESCUER DOCTRINE defendants who create peril to themselves are liable for any injury to those who come to their rescue. Under this view peril to rescuers is **reasonably foreseeable** because "peril invites rescue". And since an effort to rescue is foreseeable, peril to the rescuers is foreseeable. Courts generally agree on this, that rescuers are foreseeable plaintiffs.

For Example: Jackass recklessly crashed his car in the desert where nobody was around. Although there was nobody around at the time of the accident it was **foreseeable rescuers would come** to the aid of Jackass. Therefore, Jackass put the rescuers in danger, he owed them a duty as a result, and he is liable if they are injured.

2) *Palsgraf* and the zone of danger

Study of *Palsgraf* (*Palsgraf v. Long Island Railroad Co.* (1928) 248 N.Y. 339) is part of the traditional nonsense for first year law students. In *Palsgraf* a man carrying a package of fireworks tried to board a moving train as it left the station. Railroad employees tried to help him board the moving train. In the process the man dropped his package of fireworks and they exploded. Waiting passengers panicked, the passengers ran into a baggage scale, the scale it fell on Mrs. Palsgraf, and she was injured. Mrs. Palsgraf was about 30 feet away from the railroad workers who were trying to help the man board the train, and she was not put in any danger of being directly injured by their acts.

New York Justice Cardozo opined the railroad employees were not liable because they only had a duty of due care to plaintiffs within the "**zone of danger**", the area within which their actions created **reasonably foreseeable peril** to others. He argued Mrs. Palsgraf was not in the zone of danger so she was not owed a duty. And if she was not owed a duty, he concluded the railroad should not be liable for her injury. Cardozo's view is often paraphrased as, "A duty is only owed to <u>reasonably foreseeable plaintiffs</u>." An implied conclusion of this view is, "There is no liability to anyone who is not owed a duty."

For Example: Driver drives his car. This act creates foreseeable peril to others **in front of the car only** because it is not foreseeable driving the car could hurt anyone behind the car or to the sides of the car. Under Cardozo's view Driver could not be liable to anyone who is not in front of his moving car.

In his famous dissent, Justice Andrews argued that defendants who create **risks to anyone** have a duty to act with reasonable care, and defendants that breach that duty have done a wrongful act. Therefore, since defendants have breached their duty to someone, they **should be liable to**

everyone it causes injury. Causation in this sense is simply the application of actual and proximate cause as explained above.

Moreover, Cardozo supported the **Rescuer Doctrine**, and clearly it held that defendants were liable for acts that never put anyone but themselves in danger. Therefore, Andrews concluded that it was already established law that liability based on peril extends to foreseeable plaintiffs who are not in the zone of danger at the time of a negligent act.

Andrews' conclusion was that **if a duty is created by peril** (as opposed to other reasons) **liability has not traditionally been limited, and should not be limited to only those plaintiffs who were in the zone of danger**.

Andrews' view should NOT be understood as, "a duty to anyone creates a duty to everyone." Instead, Andrews' view was really that, "Breaching a duty based on peril creates liability to everyone actually and proximately injured whether they were the party owed the duty or not."

> **For Example:** Driver drunkenly drives his car toward Walker. Walker runs from the crosswalk to get out of the way of the speeding car, and accidentally knocks down Vick who was standing in a place of safety and not in any danger of being hit by Driver's speeding car. Under Andrews' view Driver is liable to Vick, even though Vick was not in the zone of danger, because Driver breached the duty he owed to Walker. [13]

While the opinion of Cardozo was adopted by that particular New York Court, over 80 years ago, that fact is of little or no importance. Modernly Courts probably follow the Andrews view more often than the Cardozo view, and the example immediately above is a good illustration why.

The basic finding of Palsgraf is that Cardozo said foreseeable plaintiffs have to be in the zone of danger when the defendant creates peril, and Andrews disagreed.

3) The foreseeable plaintiff

Following *Palsgraf*, the concept of liability for injury caused by creation of peril evolved more in the direction of Andrews' argument. Defendants who create peril to others are now generally liable to all **foreseeable plaintiffs**, and foreseeable plaintiffs are those who are injured as a **direct and natural consequence** of the defendant's actions and NOT just those in the **zone of danger** at the time of the breach. In other words, if defendants **proximately cause** plaintiffs' injuries, modern Courts are likely to find the plaintiffs were "**foreseeable**" and the defendants liable to them. A number of **special rules** have arisen regarding particular situations in which defendants cause plaintiffs injury.

But IT IS IMPORTANT TO UNDERSTAND **this expansion of liability** is restricted to **injury caused by breach of a duty based on peril**. It has NOT generally been applied to duties based on statute, relationship, contract and assumption. When a duty is based on those other criteria liability for breach is more likely restricted to those plaintiffs who were owed the duty in the first place.

---

[13] Note that this is exactly what happened to Mrs. Palsgraf. People who had been in the zone of danger ran away from the danger, causing Mrs. Palsgraf to be injured.

For Example: Driver has bad brakes. He pays Wrench to fix them. Wrench does not do it. If Driver crashes his car hurting Passenger, Wrench will be liable to Driver for breach of a duty based on contract, but less likely to be liable to Passenger because he did not owe Passenger a duty and did not create the peril that injured Passenger.

4) Liability to unborn children for pre-natal injury

Under the common law no duty was owed an unborn child because it was not a "person." Modernly a duty is generally owed to a **viable but unborn child** by anyone who endangers it, and **after birth** the child (or a person acting on the child's behalf) may pursue an action for injury caused by creation of peril. Some courts extend the duty to any unborn child, viable or not.

Generally, there is NO duty to an unborn child to **abort** the child if it has a birth defect.

5) Liability of automobile drivers: guest statutes

As a **general rule** automobile drivers have a **duty to passengers to drive with due care.** But under **GUEST STATUTES** adopted by some States in the mid-20th Century at the urging of auto insurance companies, passengers were deemed to have **impliedly waived** the right to bring negligence actions against the drivers of autos in which they rode. There were **two general exceptions**: Drivers had a duty to not drive while **intoxicated** or to drive **recklessly.**

Modernly few States continue to adhere to the "guest statutes." Therefore, this is not an important issue and unlikely to be tested. It is just unnecessary blather to waste your time.

6) Liability of building contractors

A building contractor that builds, renovates or repairs real property has a **duty** to **render services with due care** once construction begins. Most Courts hold contractors are liable to any party that would foreseeable be injured as a result of negligent construction.

7) Liability of hosts serving alcohol

Under the **common law** a person that served (by sale or gift) alcoholic beverages had NO DUTY to drinkers or third parties who were later injured because the **proximate cause** of the injury was the **drinking** of the beverage by the drinker and **not serving** the beverage by the server.

Modernly some courts have held that a defendant has a duty not to serve alcoholic beverages to obviously intoxicated people (guests or customers). And some States have adopted statutes defining and limiting the liability of hosts who serve alcohol to guests or customers. These are not clearly broadly adopted.

For Example: Thirsty pours 21 shots of tequila for Vick his 21st birthday. Vick drinks them all and dies. Thirsty is not liable to Vick for negligence under the common law, and would not be liable under the statutes of many States because he just **allowed** Vick to get stupid and encouraged him; he did not make Vick drink the tequila.

8) Liability of product distributors

Any person who **places a product in the stream of commerce** owes a DUTY of due care to those **reasonably foreseeable plaintiffs** that may suffer injury. This is the subject of **PRODUCT LIABILITY** which is discussed in greater detail below.

3. Premises Liability Duties

Premises liability is simply liability based on a relationship duty, but the traditional common law rules are so complicated and so often tested they deserve a separate section all by itself.

A **landlord** is someone who leases land to a **tenant**, and a **tenant** is someone who leases land from a **landlord**. A **trespasser** is a person who enters the land of the occupier without permission. **Licensees** are anyone the occupier allows onto the land for reasons other than to benefit financially or to obtain services from them. And **invitees** are people occupiers allow onto their land to gain a financial benefit or obtain services from them.

Sellers of land also have particular duties in addition to landlords and occupiers of land.

The traditional common law duties of **landlords, occupiers of land** and **sellers of land** vary between **seven classes of people**:

- **Tenants** are occupiers of land who have leased or rented the land from **landlords**;
- **Trespassing children** are children known to have entered the land of the **occupier** without permission or who are likely to trespass onto the land in the future;
- **Unknown trespassers** are people (other than trespassing children) who enter the land without permission without knowledge of the **occupier**;
- **Discovered trespassers** are trespassers the **occupier** discovers on the land;
- **Licenses** are those the **occupier** allows on the land, but not for financial benefit;
- **Invitees** are those the **occupier** asks onto the land for his financial benefit; and
- **People off the land** are people who are not on the land of the occupier but may be injured by activities on the land.

The traditional common law duties of **landlords**, **occupiers of land** and **sellers of land** also vary depending on the type of dangerous conditions on the land and activities conducted on the land.

- **Natural dangerous conditions** are things like cliffs, caves, and bodies of water;
- **Artificial dangerous conditions** are things like mines, wells, and structures;
- **Concealed dangers** of the land are hidden or not obvious dangers; and
- **Dangerous trees** are trees that are likely to fall or drop limbs.

Sometimes the duty of a party is simply to **warn** about dangerous conditions on the land. Other times the duty is to take **reasonable action** to eliminate the danger or otherwise protect other people from the dangers on the land.

--o0o--

A. Duties of Occupiers of Land

An **occupier of land** may be an owner or a tenant. Landlords are also "occupiers" of common areas they exert control over after leasing part of the land to a tenant. Occupiers of land have different duties to different classes of people.

1) Duty to trespassing children: Attractive Nuisance Doctrine

A trespasser is a person who enters the land without permission from the occupier of land.

An occupier of land has a duty of **reasonable care to protect foreseeably trespassing children** from **serious dangers** they are **unlikely to appreciate** because of their young ages. This means the occupiers of land have a duty to **search for, warn** and **protect** known or foreseeable **child trespassers** from all dangerous conditions and activities on the land. Child trespassers are foreseeable if evidence of their presence is discovered, or if the nature of the land would foreseeably attract them. This is called the **ATTRACTIVE NUISANCE DOCTRINE**.

In actions against occupiers of land based on the Attractive Nuisance Doctrine, defendants are **not allowed to raise contributory or comparative negligence** as a defense. The only allowable defense is a claim the children **assumed the risk** of injury.

> **For Example:** Tom finds a toy near the crushing machine at his mine. He doesn't search for children before he turns on the machine, crushing little Dick. Tom is liable for Dick's death because discovery of the toy put him on notice that children were around, and he had a duty to look for them before continuing any dangerous activities. The only possible defense Tom may raise is **assumption of the risk**.

The practical application of this is that every person with a swimming pool, spa, pond, pool of water, electrical transformer, or other hazardous condition on their land that might injure children will be automatically liable unless they have surrounded it with a fence that is so difficult to cross, and warnings that are so obvious, that any child who crosses it obviously has **assumed the risks**.

> **For Example:** District puts an electrical transformer in a field near a school. The transformer is surrounded by a 6 foot fence topped with 2 more feet of barbed wire. Prominent signs are posted on all sides of the transformer warning "High Voltage! Danger!" in English and Spanish. Johnny Delinquent, 11 years old, goes inside the fence, climbs on the transformer and is seriously injured. District's defense would be that it did everything reasonably possible to keep Johnny out, and he obviously **assumed the risks**. [14]

2) Duty to unknown trespassers

At common law occupiers of land have **no duty** to unforeseeable, unknown trespassers. If there is a known, dangerous condition on the land, the occupier has no duty to fix it or post warnings for trespassers the occupier does not know are on the land or are likely to come on the land.

---

[14] In other words, Johnny was either suicidal or too stupid to feel sorry for.

3) Duty to discovered, suspected or known trespassers

The occupier of land has a **duty to search for and warn foreseeable or known trespassers** before conducting dangerous activities on the land, and to use due care in conducting all activities on the land.

And the occupier has a **duty to warn** or otherwise protect foreseeable and known trespassers from known, hidden, **artificial** dangerous conditions.

"**Artificial dangerous conditions**" are mines, wells or structures as opposed to "**natural conditions**" such as caves, cliffs, trees and bodies of water.

> **For Example:** Dan knows deer hunters occasionally wander onto his land. If there is an abandoned mine they might fall into he has a duty to post a warning to protect them.

4) Duty to invitees

An **invitee** is a person the occupier of land allows on the land **to gain financial or other benefits** from the invitee's presence. It is generally a **business customer**, but not always.

The occupier of land has a **duty to search for and warn invitees** before conducting dangerous activities on the land, and to use due care in conducting all activities on the land.

And the occupier of land has a **duty to reasonably inspect the land for dangers, warn and protect** invitees from known, hidden, dangerous conditions, whether artificial or natural.

> **For Example:** Mulberry Place rents an apartment to Tom. Tom invites Paula to visit. Tom and Paula are relaxing by the pool when Paula is electrocuted by a faulty electrical plug. Paula is a social guest of Tom's but she is not injured inside his apartment. At poolside she is an **invitee** of Mulberry Place because it allowed her there to financially benefit. The pool is an amenity provided by Mulberry Place to attract tenants, and Paula is allowed there so Mulberry Place will benefit financially. Therefore, Mulberry Place had a duty to reasonably inspect for dangers and correct them.

5) Duty to licensees

A **licensee** is a person who the occupier of land allows onto the land BUT NOT for **financial benefit** or to **obtain services** from them. It is generally a **social guest**.

The occupier of land has a **duty to search for and warn licensees** before conducting dangerous activities on the land, and to use due care in conducting all activities on the land.

And the occupier of land has a **duty to warn and protect** licensees from known, hidden, dangerous conditions, whether artificial or natural. But the occupier of land had **NO duty to inspect the land** for dangerous conditions.

> **For Example:** Don invites Peter to his house for dinner. Peter is a **licensee** because he is a **social guest** and not there to give Don a financial benefit or to perform services for him. Peter slips on a banana peel and is injured. Don is liable if he knew the banana peel was on

the floor. His duty was to pick it up, or at least warn Peter not to step on it. **If the banana peel is black**, it must have been on the floor a long time and Don must have known it was there. If the banana peel is fresh, maybe Don was unaware of the danger. He had no duty to look for dangers in his home because Peter is a licensee, not an invitee.

6) Duty to people off the land

The occupier of land has a **duty to** use due care in conducting activities on the land, including activities of guests and employees, to prevent injury to people off the land. That means people near to the land but not actually on it like people passing by.

> **For Example:** Tom is walking down the road when he is shot by a bullet fired from Dick's property. Dick is liable if he was shooting or allowing others to shoot on his property because obviously they were not being careful.

And an occupier of land has a duty to **inspect and maintain artificial structures** and **inspect and eliminate dangerous trees in urban areas** to prevent injury to people off the land.

> **For Example:** Tom is walking past Dick's property when a tree falls on him. Dick is liable if the tree was obviously dead or if Dick's property is in an urban area and reasonable inspection would have revealed the danger.

An occupier of land has no duty to inspect for other natural dangers of the land.

> **For Example:** Tom is walking past Dick's property when a landslide falls on him. Dick is liable if he knew the landslide was likely and did nothing to warn others, but he had no duty to inspect for the possibility of a landslide.

7) No liability to emergency responders

Occupiers of land generally have no liability to firemen, police or other professional emergency responders if they are injured by the hazards that cause the emergency response. This rule does not apply to injury caused by intentional, wanton or reckless acts or events unrelated to the emergency response.

--o0o--

B. Duties of Landlords

A **landlord** is a party who leases land to a **tenant**. The landlord may or may not be the owner of the land. Under common law a landlord has NO DUTY to protect tenants or anyone else from dangerous conditions on the land, whether they existed at the beginning of the tenancy or developed later, subject to certain **recognized exceptions**.

1) Duty in common areas

A landlord has the **same duty as an occupier** of land, as explained above, with respect to common areas that remain under the landlord's control (hallways, lobbies, courtyards, parking lots). In effect the landlord IS the occupier of that part of the land.

Traditionally there was NO DUTY to protect tenants and others from **criminal acts** in those areas but some courts have held a landlord has a duty to take **reasonable precautions** when **aware of prior crimes** and that there is a **predictable risk** to tenants.

> **For Example:** Mark manages an apartment complex. Tenants report a suspicious character has been loitering in the parking garage. Some courts hold Mark has a duty to warn the tenants. Mark may also have a duty to reasonably inspect to determine how the suspect has been getting into the garage.

2) Duty when leasing for public use

A landlord leasing land for purposes that will allow **public admission** has a **duty to inspect and repair** at the time of lease **unless he reasonably believes** the necessary precautions will be taken by the tenant before the public is admitted. If the tenant agrees to repair dangerous conditions before the public will be admitted the landlord is relieved of that duty.

3) Duty to people off the land

A landlord has the **same duty as an occupier** of land to people off of the land as explained below. Leasing the land to a tenant does not change this duty and liability.

> **For Example:** Larry owns a rental house with a big dead tree in the yard that is likely to fall on pedestrians walking past on the sidewalk. He has a duty to have the tree removed. He is not relieved of that duty by simply renting the house to Bubba.

4) Liability for promised or negligent repairs

A landlord who **negligently repairs** property is directly liable to anyone injured as a result after the land is leased to a tenant. And a landlord who **promises to repair** leased property but does not is liable to anyone injured if the failure creates an **unreasonable risk of harm** to others. This may be viewed as a **contractual** or **assumed** duty more than a **relationship** duty.

5) Duty to disclose known, concealed dangers

A landlord has a duty to disclose **known, concealed, dangerous conditions** to tenants at the time of lease. That duty, and the liability arising from it, continues until the tenant has had time to otherwise discover the condition.

> **For Example:** Larry rents a storage shed to Tom. At the time he tells Tom the electrical wiring is defective and needs to be repaired. If Tom rents the shed anyway, he has assumed the risks. If Larry had not disclosed the dangerous condition he would continue to be liable **until Tom had possession long enough to discover the danger himself**. But after Tom has possession long enough to discover the problem and does nothing to repair it, he has **assumes the risks** at that time.

--o0o--

C. Duties of Land Sellers

Under traditional common law **land sellers** have a duty to **warn buyers** about known, dangerous conditions on the land, and to **protect people off the land** from known dangerous conditions on the land until the buyer has adequate time to inspect the premises and take corrective measures. Other than that, sellers of real property have no other duties to protect buyers or third parties from dangerous conditions on the land under traditional common law.

--o0o--

D. Modern Trends in Premises Liability

The traditional common law rules explained above are heavily tested. But modernly many Courts have adopted a **more general approach**.

Occupiers of land are increasingly seen to have a **general duty** to reasonably **inspect** and **maintain** real property, to take reasonable steps to **eliminate known hazards**, to reasonably **warn** and **act to protect all people** who come onto the land, and to use **reasonable care** so that **activities on the land do not harm** others.

4. Breaches of Duties

To establish a cause of action for negligence plaintiffs must prove defendants not only had a duty to act with due care but that they have also **breached** that duty. A breach of duty is a **failure to act as reasonably necessary under the same circumstances**. This is typically called the **standard of due care**.

--o0o--

A. Reasonably Necessary Action

Acting "**as reasonably necessary**" means the **more dangerous** the perils, **the more the defendant should do** to protect others from them. If **perils are easy to eliminate**, the **defendant should eliminate them**. If perils **cannot be eliminated**, the defendant should **warn** about them.

--o0o--

B. Extent of Liability Created by Breach

Breach of duty does not make defendants liable to everybody in the universe. Legal **liability** for a breach of duty <u>generally is limited to the plaintiffs who were owed that duty</u>. There are some **generally recognized exceptions** to this rule:

- Breach of a duty based on **peril** often makes defendants liable to all who are actually and proximately caused **personal injury** or **property damage** even if they were not in the "**zone of danger**" and therefore, not owed a duty at the time of the breach. This is the argument presented by Andrews in *Palsgraf.*

- Under the **Rescuer Doctrine** defendants are generally liable to **amateur rescuers** (excluding "professional rescuers") who are injured coming to their aid or to the aid of others they have put in peril even if they were not owed a duty at the time of the breach.
- Generally, defendants are liable in **wrongful death** actions to plaintiffs who were financially dependent on people wrongfully killed by the defendant's breach even if they were not owed a duty at the time of the breach.
- Defendants may be liable to **bystanders, friends** and **relatives** of accident victims for **negligent infliction of emotional distress** (NIED).

  For Example: Nurse is hired by Dotter to care for Invalid. She owes Dotter a duty based on contract and a duty to Invalid as an intended third party beneficiary of that contract. Invalid has two dependents, Dotter and Sonny. Invalid has also promised to give Benny a gift of $1 million. Nurse fails to meet her duty of due care, and Invalid suffers as a result. That causes Invalid's creditors to go unpaid, and Benny does not get his gift. Nurse is only liable to **Invalid** and **Dotter** in most cases because her duty is based on <u>contract</u>. But <u>if Invalid dies</u> Nurse may also be liable to Sonny in a <u>wrongful death action</u>, even though she did not owe Sonny a duty of due care for any reason. But she is <u>never</u> going to be liable to Invalid's creditors or to Benny because her duty based on contract does not create a liability that extends to them.

--o0o--

C. Standards of Due Care

The **standard of due care** is the behavior required of a person with a duty to act.

1) The average adult standard of care

The general **standard of due care** required of a person with a duty to act is the **average adult standard of care**. That means defendants have a duty to exercise the level of care and caution that a **reasonably prudent adult** of **average intelligence, education and experience** would exercise under the **same circumstances**. [15]

There are **exceptions** when this general standard does not apply, as explained below.

2) Statutory standards of care

If a **statute expressly** defines a **standard of behavior** or establishes a standard of behavior by **implication**, AND the purpose of the statute is to **protect a defined class** of people from a **defined type of injury** it defines a **statutory standard of care**.

3) The average child standard of care

The **standard of due care for children** is to act the way **reasonably prudent children of average intelligence with the same age and experience** act **UNLESS they are engaged in adult activities**.

---

[15] Note that what the "average" person does is generally going to be "reasonable". So if the "average" driver drives five miles an hour over the speed limit, that is not "unreasonable", even though it violates the law.

But if a child is engaged in **adult activities** they are held to the **average adult standard of care**.

> **For Example:** Ten-year-old Buddy accidentally runs over Jimmy with his father's truck. Buddy is held to the **average adult standard of care** because "driving a truck" is an **adult activity**.

4) The medical standard of care

Courts are split concerning the acceptable level of medical care. Some Courts hold the **standard of due care for medical professionals** is the **<u>national</u> standard of acceptable medical care** and other Courts hold it is the **<u>local</u> standard of acceptable medical care**.

5) Skilled professional standards of care

People who are, or claim to be, skilled professionals are held to the **average skilled professional standard of care**. That means defendants have a duty to exercise the level of care and caution that a **reasonably prudent person with the same or claimed level of training** would exercise under the **same circumstances**. [16]

6) Physically disabled standard of care

People who are **physically disabled** (not mentally impaired) have a duty to exercise the level of care and caution that a **reasonably prudent person with the same physical disability** would exercise under the **same circumstances**.

7) Emergency standard of care

People who are **confronted by an emergency** have a duty to exercise the level of care and caution that a **reasonably prudent average person** would exercise in the **same emergency situation**.

8) No exception for mental impairment

There is **no lower standard of care for people** who are **mentally impaired** for any reason, whether it is low intelligence, intoxication, ignorance, or stupidity.

--o0o--

D. Breaches of Statutory Standards of Care

If a statute is intended to protect a **class of people** from a **type of harm** it establishes both a **statutory duty** and a **statutory standard of care**.

If a defendant **violates the statute** and it **causes** (meaning **actual** and **proximate cause**) a plaintiff that is **in the class** to suffer **the type of injury** the statute was intended to prevent, the defendant is held to be **NEGLIGENT PER SE**. The only other thing the plaintiff has to prove is the amount of damage caused.

---

[16] Note that this means people who lie about their qualifications are held to a higher standard of behavior than they are actually trained for.

> **For Example:** A statute prohibits children from riding in the back of pick-up trucks to prevent injuries. The **statutory standard of care** is to not drive with children in the back of a truck. Driver drives with his child Sonny in the back of his truck, both violating the law and breaching the standard of due care. Sonny falls out and gets hurt. Driver is **negligent per se** because Sonny is a **child** (the class to be protected) and he suffered the type of injury the statute was intended to prevent.

--o0o--

E. Breaches in Failing to Fully Inform Medical Patients

Medical professionals have a **duty to obtain fully informed consent** from patients before performing **procedures that pose material risks**. They must fully inform the patient of the **material risks** and **benefits** of both the **proposed procedure** and **alternative means of treatment**.

If medical professionals perform procedures without fully informing the patient, and the **procedure causes injury**, they are **liable for negligence** subject to **two exceptions**.

They are NOT liable if the **patient would have consented to the same procedure anyway**, even if they had been fully informed.

And they are NOT liable if they **deliberately and reasonably withheld** the information fro the plaintiff **to protect the patient's mental or physical health**.

> **For Example:** Doctor Hack does a radical mastectomy on Buffy without telling her that chemotherapy was a good alternative. She suffers injury. Buffy sues for medical malpractice saying that if she had known of the alternative she "might not have consented" to the mastectomy. Doctor Hack will NOT be liable if Buffy only says she "might not have consented" because her burden is to prove she would not have consented but for Dr. Hack's negligence. Otherwise she cannot prove she has suffered any injury with certainty.

--o0o--

F. Shifting Burden of Proof with Res Ipsa Loquitur

Plaintiffs normally have the burden of proving defendants were negligent, and the acts the defendants did to cause the plaintiff's injury. But in some situations there is NO EVIDENCE to prove which of several possible defendants injured the plaintiffs.

> **For Example:** Pete is walking down the street when a box of merchandise falls on him out of the second floor window of Defendant Warehousing Company. There were ten Ace employees working on the second floor moving boxes about, but none of them will say they saw what happened and they have no idea what caused the box to fall out of the window. Obviously someone working for Defendant accidentally or deliberately dropped the box on Pete. But how can he prove it?

And in some cases thee is NO EVIDENCE to prove what the defendants did to cause the plaintiffs' injuries.

For Example: Don's Auto Repair catches on fire one Sunday when nobody is around. The fire burns down Paul's Shop next door. There are no witnesses and fire investigators cannot determine what caused the fire. Obviously something at Don's Auto Repair caused the fire, but how can Paul prove it was Don's fault?

In these cases the plaintiff pleads **res ipsa loquitur**. That means "the facts speak for themselves" and it allows the plaintiff to **shift the burden of proof** to the defendants. Instead of the plaintiff having to prove the defendants WERE negligent, the plaintiffs have to prove they were NOT negligent.

Res ipsa loquitur is only allowed when 1) the facts show or strongly suggest **someone was negligent**, 2) the plaintiff **clearly suffered injury**, and 3) the plaintiff **had little or no control over the situation** that caused the injury. That means the plaintiffs were clearly not the cause of their own injuries.

For Example: Pat and Dick are in an auto accident at an intersection. Pat accuses Dick of negligently running a red light and causing the accident. Dick denies liability and claims Pat was the one who ran the red light. Pat sues Dick. Pat has the burden of proving Dick was negligent, but he has NO WITNESSES. Can Pat shift the burden of proof to Dick by citing **res ipsa loquitur**? No, because Pat had some control over the situation and may have caused the accident himself.

But consider this alternative:

For Example: Pat and Dick are in an auto accident at an intersection. Frank, a passenger in Dick's car, is badly injured. Pat accuses Dick of negligently running a red light and causing the accident. Dick denies liability and claims Pat was the one who ran the red light. Frank sues both of them. Frank normally has the burden of proving Pat was negligent, Dick was negligent, or both of them were negligent. But clearly one of them was negligent. So Frank just sues both of them, cites **res ipsa loquitur**, and shifts the burden to both of them to prove who ran the red light. If neither of them can prove the other was at fault, both are **substantial factors** in causing Frank's injury and both of them are **jointly and severally liable**, as those terms were explained earlier.

--o0o--

G. Negligent Entrustment

When defendants ENTRUST **authority, possession, power**, **opportunity** or **control** over events or objects that pose reasonably foreseeable dangers to others, they create **reasonably foreseeable peril** to others.

For Example: Owen loans Driver his car. Since driving a car creates reasonably foreseeable perils to others, **loaning the car** also creates reasonably foreseeable perils to others.

As a result, the defendants have a **duty** to exercise caution and only ENTRUST such powers to a trustworthy individual. If they **breach that duty** by giving power to someone whom no reasonable person would ever trust with such powers, they will be liable for **negligent entrustment**.

> **For Example:** Owen loans Driver his car knowing that Driver is a very reckless driver. Since no reasonable person would loan their car to a reckless driver, Owen is liable for any harm his act of loaning the car causes.

But when defendants SELL or GIVE **authority, possession, power, opportunity**, or **control** to others liability is not so clear. The standard for negligence is what an "average reasonable person" would do, and a "reasonable person" is far more likely to sell or give something to a reckless or unreliable person than to "entrust" something to them.

> **For Example:** Driver offers to buy a car from Joe's Used Cars after telling the salesman he needs a car because he got drunk and wrecked his last one. Every used car salesman in the world would be more than willing to sell Driver another car, even if there was a good chance he would wreck it too. And no jury would ever find that to be "negligent entrustment" because "selling" a car is not considered to be an "entrustment" at all.

--o0o--

H. Negligent Contracting

Negligent contracting is a particular type of **negligent entrustment**. Defendants who contract with independent contractors are generally **not vicariously liable** for tortuous acts of the contractors, but they may be **directly liable** for their own failure to carefully investigate the qualifications of the contractor because in hiring the contractor the defendant often gives the contractor **authority, possession, power** and **control** over events that pose reasonably foreseeable dangers to others.

> **For Example:** George contracts with Blackwater to run his prison camp at Gitmo even though Blackwater has performed negligently in the past. George is NOT vicariously liable for Blackwater's negligence or even its intentional acts (e.g. torture, waterboarding), because Blackwater is an independent contractor. But George IS **directly liable** for any future torts by Blackwater because he **negligently contracted** with Blackwater, thereby **negligently entrusting** it with the authority, power, possession of the facility, opportunity, and control that enables it to commit those torts.

--o0o--

I. Gross Negligence

Gross negligence means a person with a **duty to protect others from extreme risks deliberately breached** that duty.

> **For Example:** Dee is hired by Ford to test car airbags. She has a duty based on **contract** to test the bags. But she deliberately marks many of them to be "OK" without ever testing them, breaching her duty and causing extreme risks to future passengers.

--o0o--

J. Recklessness

Recklessness means a person deliberately created extreme risks to others.

> **For Example:** Dee is hired by Ford to test car airbags. She has a duty based on **contract** to test the bags. Instead, she deliberately punches holes in many of the bags, making them dysfunctional and creating extreme risks to future passengers. [17]

5. Causation for Negligence

To prove negligence, plaintiffs must prove the defendants' breach of duty was the **cause** of their injury as with every other tort. Causation, including **actual cause** or **substantial factor**, and **proximate cause** was explained in Chapter 1. There is no point repeating it all here, but you might want to go back to review it there.

6. Damages for Negligence

Tort remedies were explained earlier in Chapter 3. It is traditional to say that plaintiffs in negligence actions always have a burden of proving the **damages** caused by the defendant's breach of duty. This is true in the vast majority of situations but not exactly correct. The plaintiff has a burden of proving the negligent acts of the defendant caused a **wrongful result**. In the vast majority of negligence situations the "wrongful result" is that the plaintiff suffered injury. Therefore, it is almost always correct to say the plaintiff must prove **damages**. But it is still possible the negligent act of the defendant would create **unjust enrichment**.

> **For Example:** HMO treats Juan for a skin rash with Calamine. Reasonable medical doctors would treat him with Expensocillin, because Calamine is much less effective. But HMO saves itself $1,000 by using the cheaper alternative. HMO breaches its duty to Juan, causing him to have a rash for an additional week. Juan has a right to a money judgment for $1,000 in **legal restitution** (not damages) to prevent HMO from reaping an unjust enrichment from its breach of duty.

Punitives are **never awarded for negligent acts**, unless there is proof of **gross negligence** or **recklessness**. That was explained earlier in Chapter 3.

Award of a money judgment is almost always an adequate remedy in a negligence action, so **equitable remedies are seldom an issue**.

7. Defenses to Negligence Causes of Action

As with any cause of action, the defendant may raise a **passive defense** by claiming that the plaintiff has failed to prove the necessary elements of the cause of action. But when the plaintiff has presented a prima facie case, there are three (and only three) **affirmative defenses** to a claim of negligence. They are **assumption of the risk, contributory negligence** and **comparative negligence.**

---

[17] As irrational as this seems, it is typical of the wacky things people actually do.

In addition to these defenses, the common law recognized traditional **immunities** from suits for negligence for **family members** (e.g. husband v. wife, parent v. child), **government entities** (e.g. barriers to suits against states) and **charities**. These immunities have substantially been eliminated and do not merit much discussion other than as a historical note.

--o0o--

A. Assumption of the Risk

Under the common law, assumption of the risk is a **complete bar to recovery** for negligence.

Assumption of the risk may either be a **primary** assumption of the risk by an **agreement** or a **secondary** assumption of the risk by **voluntary action.**

1) Primary (consensual) assumption of the risk

Primary assumption of risk means the plaintiff 1) **expressly** or 2) **impliedly agreed** to assume the risk of injury posed by the defendant's acts or failure to act and the agreement was 3) **not void by public policy**.

> **For Example:** Tourist signs up for a kayaking tour on the Wailua River in Kauai. He is required to sign a "waiver" acknowledging he is aware of the risks posed by kayaking.

An **express agreement** is one the plaintiff signs or orally agrees to which states acceptance of known risks, and an **implied agreement** is indicated by the plaintiff proceeding after **reading and understanding** a written statement limiting liability. There is also an implied agreement if the plaintiff enters the defendant's premises or receives services after being given **a statement of liability limitations** and being **given reasonable notice** of its contents, even if the statement is not read by the plaintiff.

A primary assumption of risks is only a valid defense if the **injuries suffered are within the scope** of the agreement **as it was understood and contemplated by the plaintiff**.

> **For Example:** Owen hands his car keys to Valet, a parking lot attendant, and gets a ticket that says, "Patron assumes all risks of damage to cars in parking lot." Valet is still liable for **the damage he causes to the car himself** if Owen understands the risk he "assumed" was that **third parties** might enter the lot and damage the car.

An agreement limiting liability is **void by public policy** if it:

- Attempts to **eliminate a duty of due care imposed by statute or public policy**,
- Is the result of **undue influence, oppression or duress**, or is
- Otherwise **inherently unfair**.

2) Secondary (voluntary) assumption of the risk

A **secondary assumption of risk** takes place when the plaintiff 1) **knows and appreciates the risks** and 2) **voluntarily chooses** to subject him or herself to the risks. In many jurisdictions the plaintiff's decision to subject himself to risks must be **unreasonable**. In others it does not matter if the decision is unreasonable or not. If the risk is unreasonable, the act is negligent, and if comparative negligence has been adopted (discussed below) secondary assumption of the risk no longer acts as a complete bar to recovery.

> **For Example:** Hans goes skiing. He goes to the top of the mountain, heads down a triple-black-diamond run, goes off a cliff and is badly injured. Hans is generally going to be found to have **voluntarily assumed the risks** clearly posed by his own actions.

3) The Fireman's Rule

The **Fireman's Rule** is a narrow and special application of assumption of the risk. Firemen, policemen, and others who are professionally trained to deal with hazardous situations are generally held to have **assumed the risks** of their professions. Therefore, they **cannot recover damages for injuries suffered while responding to emergencies caused by the negligent acts of others**.

But the Fireman's Rule does not bar rescue personnel from recovering damages for intentional acts, reckless acts, failure to reasonably give warning of known hidden dangers, or injury suffered from negligent acts that are not the cause of emergency personnel going the location of a hazardous situation.

> **For Example:** Fireman Frank responds to a fire caused by Dan, and he accidentally burns to death when the fire rages out of control. Frank's family can bring a tort action (wrongful death suit) against Dan if he intentionally set the fire as an act of arson. They cannot bring an action if the fire was caused by Dan's negligence.

--o0o--

B. Contributory Negligence

Contributory negligence is **negligence by a plaintiff** that helps cause the event that injures the plaintiff or else causes the plaintiff's injury to be greater that it otherwise would have been. Traditionally, **contributory negligence** was a **complete bar** to recovery.

> **For Example:** Driver runs a stop sign and hits Walker who stepped off the curb without looking. Under the **contributory negligence** rule Walker cannot recover anything from Driver for his injuries because he was **also negligent.**

The effects of the contributory negligence defense were so rigid and harsh that Courts constructed a number of **saving doctrines** that could be used on an ad hoc basis to avoid inequity in different situations. Since these "saving doctrines" were created by various cases with various fact patterns, they ended up being something of a "patchwork" of concepts that vary widely between States. This patchwork of Court decisions created a rather silly set of rules.

1) Last Clear Chance Doctrine

The **Last Clear Chance Doctrine** held that contributory negligence by a plaintiff was NOT a complete bar to recovery IF the defendant had a last clear chance to avoid the accident that injured the plaintiff and failed to do so.

> **For Example:** Walker starts crossing the street without looking, so he is negligent. Driver comes driving along without looking. Walker runs for safety but is hit anyway. Under the **last clear chance** rule Walker is not totally barred from recovery because Driver was the one who had the **last clear chance to avoid the accident.**

NOT IF BOTH PARTIES EQUALLY INATTENTIVE. Courts held that the **last clear chance rule** did NOT apply if BOTH the defendant and plaintiff are unaware of an impending accident because they were **equally at fault and neither has a "last chance".**

> **For Example:** Walker starts crossing the street without looking. Driver is driving without looking and the accident happens before either of them sees the other. Walker is totally barred by contributory negligence because **neither was paying attention**.

NOT IF DEFENDANT HELPLESS. Courts held that the **last clear chance doctrine** did NOT apply if the **defendant was helpless to avoid the accident** because of some **prior negligence** (rather than current negligence) on his own part.

> **For Example:** Plaintiff Walker starts crossing the street without looking. Driver sees Walker but **cannot avoid the accident** because his car has bad brakes. Although Driver is negligent for having bad brakes, the negligence itself makes it impossible to avoid the accident. Therefore, Driver has **no chance** to avoid the accident and cannot be said to have had a "last clear chance" to avoid the accident. Since Driver did not have a "last clear chance", Walker is barred from recovery by contributory negligence.

WHEN PLAINTIFF IS AWARE AND HELPLESS. Courts have been split in applying the last clear chance rule when negligent **plaintiffs were aware of the dangers they faced but were helpless to avoid injury**. Some Courts have held plaintiffs are not barred by contributory negligence if the **defendants were also aware of the dangers and <u>could have avoided</u> the accident.** Other Courts have held plaintiffs are not barred by contributory negligence if the **defendants <u>should have been aware of the dangers</u> and avoided the accidents**.

> **For Example:** Walker starts crossing the street without looking. Then Walker **sees Driver coming**, but he **cannot avoid the accident**. Under one view Walker can claim Driver had the last clear chance because Driver **should have been watching where he was going.** Under the other view Walker can only claim Driver had the last clear chance if Driver **actually saw** Walker in time to stop.

2) Avoidable Injury Doctrine

The inequitable result of the contributory negligence rule also led many Courts to hold that contributory negligence is only a partial bar when negligence by the plaintiff **did not actually cause the accident** but only **caused more severe injuries** that otherwise would have been the case. This is generally called the **avoidable injury doctrine** and when it is applied the Court will apportion the damages based on fault between the plaintiff and the defendant in much the same manner as if the State had adopted a "pure comparative negligence" approach.

> **For Example:** Tom carelessly hits a car carrying Dick and Harry. It is all Tom's fault. But Dick is not wearing his seat belt. And if he had been wearing his seat belt he would have suffered minor injury ($1,000). But because he was not wearing the seatbelt he suffers major injury ($100,000). Harry is wearing his seatbelt and suffers only a concussion ($1,000) but he does not go to a doctor. A day later he has a seizure that could have been avoided, and he has $100,000 in medical bills as a result. Since the accident was all Tom's fault, Dick and Harry are not contributorily negligent for causing the accident. But since their acts increased the severity of their own injuries then are contributorily negligent for causing some of their injuries. If the **avoidable injury doctrine** were applied Tom would only be liable to each for $1,000 rather than all of the medical expenses that were caused by their own negligence.

3) Both-Ways Rule

If a defendant is **vicariously liable** for negligence the defendant can always raise contributory negligence as a defense if the plaintiff was partly at fault for the accident. But in the same way a defendant can also claim a plaintiff was **vicariously negligent** if a third party in an agency relationship with the plaintiff was partially at fault for the accident. This concept is called **the "both ways" rule**.

> **For Example:** Tom and Dick are business partners on a business trip. While Dick is driving he collides with Harry in a State where contributory negligence as a complete defense. Tom, Dick and Harry are all injured. The Court determines Dick was 5% at fault for the accident and Harry was 95% at fault. Tom is not at fault at all. Harry cannot recover against Dick, and Dick cannot recover against Harry, because each was partially at fault and contributory negligence bars each from recovering. BUT under the "both ways" rule Tom also could not recover against Harry because his partner, Dick, was a little bit at fault for causing the accident. Tom is deemed to be **vicariously negligent** because his partner, Dick, was a little bit negligent.

The "both ways" rule has been **repudiated by many courts** because of the inequitable results illustrated by the preceding example. Most States have now abandoned contributory negligence as a defense in favor of **comparative negligence** rules.

--o0o--

C. Comparative Negligence

Comparative negligence is a statutory rule that allows plaintiffs bringing claims of negligence to recover, in some circumstances, even if they were **partially at fault** for their own injury. It is also called "**comparative fault**". Under comparative negligence rules the plaintiffs' injury awards are proportionally reduced to reflect the plaintiffs' comparative fault in causing their own injuries.

Most States now follow this approach, with two basic approaches: **pure comparative negligence** and **modified comparative negligence**.

1) Pure Comparative Negligence

Under the **pure comparative negligence** approach plaintiffs may recover for **any portion** of their injuries that is caused by the defendant.

> **For Example:** Dick collides with Harry and is 10% at fault. Dick's damages are $100,000 and Harry's are $200,000, so total damages are $300,000. Each party would be a complainant against the other. Dick would be responsible for 10% of the total injuries ($30,000). He would be awarded a judgment for the balance of his injuries ($70,000) from Harry.

2) Modified Comparative Negligence

Under a **modified comparative negligence** approach plaintiffs can only recover if they were **less responsible for the accident** than the defendants. The exact approach varies by State. If the plaintiffs are more at fault for the accident than the defendants, the plaintiffs recover nothing, and **contributory negligence** effectively applies as a complete bar to recovery. This automatically means that plaintiffs are barred from recovery if they are over 50% at fault for their own injuries.

--o0o--

D. Egg-Shell and Negligent Plaintiffs Compared

The difference between egg-shell plaintiffs and plaintiffs that have been "contributorily or comparatively negligent" or have "assumed the risks" is that <u>egg-shell plaintiffs are vulnerable due to forces beyond their control</u>, through no negligence of their own.

Chapter 8: Negligent Infliction of Emotional Distress

Although "Negligence" and "Negligence Infliction of Emotional Distress (NIED)" sound very similar, they are actually distinctively different causes of action and should not be confused. If a defendant **commits any tort against a plaintiff**, whether it is negligence or some other tort, the defendant is always liable for all emotional distress that causes the plaintiff. That is just part of the "general damages".

But if a defendant commits a tort against some OTHER person who is NOT the plaintiff, and the plaintiff claims that seeing the tort take place or hearing about it afterward caused them severe emotional distress, that is a cause of action for NIED.

Negligent Infliction of Emotional Distress (NIED) is a cause of action seeking damages for emotional distress suffered by **bystanders, witnesses, rescuers, friends** and **relatives** of tort victims who were not directly harmed by the torts themselves and only claim they suffered INDIRECT INJURY because they saw the torts occur, because of what they saw after the torts occurred, or they heard about the torts after it happened.

> **For Example:** Al hears on the TV news that OJ is very rich and he killed his wife. Al sues OJ for NIED claiming he is so upset by what he heard he can't sleep at night.

To discourage frivolous actions based on false claims of NIED the Courts have established various minimum requirements a plaintiff must prove. In some States NIED plaintiffs must prove they suffered **physical contact** of some sort with the accident itself (i.e. splattered with blood and gore). Other States have rejected the "physical contact" requirement as being too rigid.

In general, NIED plaintiffs are required to prove the following elements:

1. The **defendant's tortuous acts injured some other party**.
2. The plaintiff suffered **severe emotional distress** as a result.
3. The plaintiff had such a **close relationship to event or the injured party** that the defendant should be liable for the severe emotional distress the plaintiff has suffered.

The "close relationship" is often referred to as a "nexus". It is the most difficult element to prove in an NIED action. Generally, it requires the plaintiff to prove:

1. Either the plaintiff **saw other parties injured** or **came to the scene immediately afterward and witnessed the injury that had occurred**; OR
2. The plaintiff was a **very close friend or relative** of the person injured and **saw the injury occur**, saw the injured person **immediately after** the event or learned of the injury **immediately after** it occurred.

Note that the tort committed by the defendant against the "original victim" does not have to be negligence. It can be an intentional tort like a battery. The "negligence" is the plaintiffs' claim the defendants were "negligent" for committing torts that made them upset.

Chapter 9: Products Liability

Products liability is a peculiar tort cause of action because it is a complaint with four or five possible tort arguments.

The basic rule is this: Any person who **releases** an **unreasonably dangerous** product **into the stream of commerce** may be liable for the injuries caused based on causes of action based on five very different theories: 1) **battery**, 2) **negligence**, 3) **breach of express warranty**, 4) **breach of implied warranty** or 5) **strict liability** in tort.

When a product liability (PL) cause of action is based on **battery**, it is an **intentional tort** claim. When it is based on negligence alone, it is a **negligence** claim **based on a peril duty**. When it is based on breach of warranty, it is a **negligence** claim **based on a contract duty**. And when it is a **strict liability** claim, it is a based on a **strict liability** argument.

1. Unreasonably Dangerous Products

The threshold element of every PL claim is that the plaintiff has a burden of proving the product in question was **unreasonably dangerous** when it was released into the stream of commerce. The "stream of commerce" means the **sales chain** from the manufacturer, to the wholesaler, to the retailer, and to the consumer who might yet give it as a gift or sell it to someone else.

A product is **unreasonably dangerous** if it 1) is **dangerous in some way** when **used in a foreseeable manner** and the danger is 2) **unnecessary** or 3) the **dangers far outweigh the potential benefits** of the product, or 4) the dangers **could be easily or cheaply reduced or eliminated** without destroying the utility of the product. This is a "balance" test.

Products are NOT unreasonably dangerous simply because the injure someone.

> **For Example:** Cutter cuts himself with a kitchen knife. It is NOT an unreasonably dangerous product because 1) knives have utility, 2) knives must be sharp to be functional, 3) reasonable people are **aware** knives are sharp, and 3) the **benefits from having sharp knives outweigh the dangers** they pose. So everyone knows knives are sharp, and that danger cannot be eliminated without making he knife dull and useless.

Plaintiffs with product liability claims have the burden of proving the produce was **unreasonably dangerous** at the time it is released into the stream of commerce by the defendant by being **sold, leased** or **given away.** The product is removed from the stream of commerce, and not released into the stream of commerce, if the defendant **discards** it or it is **taken** from the defendant.

A product that appears safe at the time of release is still unreasonably dangerous if it is likely (not just possible) it will **be modified** or **misused** in so that it becomes unreasonably dangerous.

> **For Example:** LawnCo sells a lawn mower that becomes **very dangerous** if a safety shield is removed, and the mower is designed in a manner that makes it easy and likely it will later be modified in that way. The mower is unreasonably dangerous at the time of sale unless there are **adequate warnings** posted on the mower. It is not adequate to put

warnings of serious danger in an "owner's manual" because it is likely the manual will be separated from the product, or the user will not read the warnings in a manual.

2. Proof of "Defective" is Irrelevant

Many professors and legal writers teach that product liability plaintiffs must prove the products that caused their injuries were **defective**. This is totally wrong. The plain English meaning of "defective" is that a product was not made as intended by the maker or does not work as intended. It does not mean **unreasonably dangerous** at all. Many defective products are simply not dangerous.

> **For Example:** A motorcycle that will not run is defective. But it is also safer than a motorcycle that is not defective. Nobody has ever been hurt by a motorcycle that does not run.

Product liability plaintiffs must prove the product that injured them was **unreasonably dangerous**, and many unreasonably dangerous products are made exactly as the manufacturer intended, and work as they intended as well.

> **For Example:** The Ford Pinto was an unreasonably dangerous product, but it was made exactly the way Ford engineers and Ford lawyers intended for it to be made. They knew it was going to burn some people to death, and they knew they could prevent that if they spent $5 more per auto. But they calculated the odds and decided they would make more by making an unreasonably dangerous car than it would cost them later in lawsuits. So they made and sold the car exactly as they intended.

So the word "defective" does not always mean "unreasonably dangerous", and the term "unreasonably dangerous" does not always mean "defective". Saying "defective" to mean "unreasonably dangerous" is simply a pointless corruption of the English language.

3. Use of Res Ipsa Loquitur to Prove Causation

When a product is unreasonably dangerous because of a **defect of unknown origin** it may be impossible for the plaintiff to prove **who caused** the defect, **what caused** the defect, or **when** the defect was created.

Under the doctrine of RES IPSA LOQUITUR **the burden of proving causation can be shifted** to the defendants if plaintiffs can show:

- **The product was unreasonably dangerous** when they were injured;
- **The unreasonable dangers** of the product **caused their injury**; and
- **They had little or no control** over the product before they were injured.

> **For Example:** Manny manufactures a tire and sells it to retailer Moe who in turn installs the tire on the car of consumer Jack. Jack is injured while driving because the tire had a hidden "sidewall defect" and suddenly "blew out". **The product was unreasonably dangerous** because it had a "sidewall defect". The dangers of the product caused Jack's

injury because it "blew out". And Jack had little or no control over the product IF <u>the tire blew out when it was brand new</u>. But if Jack had driven on the tire for some time before it "blew out" he had considerable control over the tire and might not be able to prove he did not cause the problem himself by failing to maintain it properly.

4. Products Liability for Battery

Battery is an intentional tort as explained earlier. Defendants who **intentionally** release **unreasonably dangerous** products into the stream of commerce for the purpose of causing a "touching" or with knowledge with reasonable certainty it will cause a "touching" are liable for **battery** if the "touching" is harmful or offensive.

> **For Example:** Luigi sells bottles of oil labeled "Pure Olive Oil" that he has deliberately adulterated with peanut oil. Luigi either intends for consumers to eat the oil (a "touching") or else he knows with reasonable certainty that will occur. Therefore, Luigi intentionally acts to cause a "touching". Eater consumes the oil and suffers a severe allergic reaction. Luigi is liable for a battery.

5. Products Liability for Negligence

Anyone who carelessly puts an unreasonably dangerous product into the stream of commerce will be liable for **negligence**. The elements of negligence must be proven, but they are relatively easy to establish. However, the required elements to prove negligence in a product liability case are **significantly different from proof in other negligence actions**.

--o0o--

A. Duty

Everyone **<u>has a duty</u>** to **not release an unreasonably dangerous product** into the stream of commerce. That is the ONLY duty rule in product liability law.

--o0o--

B. Breach

Defendants **breach** their duty if they do release unreasonably dangerous products into the stream of commerce **knowing** or **having cause to suspect** the product poses unreasonable dangers or **failing to reasonably inspect** the product when inspection **would have revealed the dangers** posed. That is the breach rule in product liability law.

C. Causation

The release must be the **actual and proximate cause** of injury. The defendant would be liable for the same types of injuries as in any other negligence action. Causation rules in product liability law are exactly the same as for any other tort.

--o0o--

D. Damages

The defendant is liable for **personal injury** and **property damage** caused by the unreasonable dangers posed by the product, as well as any **economic damages** (e.g. lost profits, lost wages) caused by the personal injury and property damage.

> **For Example:** Hawker, a grocer, sells a can of soup containing a pebble to Soupy. Soupy breaks a tooth on the pebble when eating the soup. Hawker is NOT liable on a negligence theory because 1) he did not know and 2) did not have reason to suspect there was a pebble in the soup and 3) there was no reasonable means by which he could inspect the soup inside the can.

--o0o--

E. Proper Plaintiffs

Under the holding of *MacPherson v. Buick* and subsequent cases the duty extends to **all foreseeable plaintiffs** that are "likely" to be endangered by the product. Any plaintiff would seem to be foreseeable if he or she suffers the **direct and natural injuries** posed by the product's unreasonably dangerous condition.

--o0o--

F. Defenses

The regular negligence defenses of **assumption of the risk**, **contributory negligence**, **comparative negligence** and **avoidable injury** are all possible defenses to a products liability claim based on negligence. In addition the defendant may claim the product was misused.

> **For Example:** Bubba, who weighs 300 pounds, buys a flimsy, cheap ladder that has no load rating. The ladder starts sagging and creaking as soon as he starts using it. He ignores the danger signs until the ladder collapses. The ladder was unreasonably dangerous because it should have had a maximum load warning, but Bubba was also **negligent** and may even have **assumed the risks** of injury by continuing to use the ladder. The defendants may also claim he **misused** the product.

6. Products Liability for Breach of Express Warranty

If the defendant **expressly represents a product is fit** for the use that causes the plaintiff injury, a claim for injury caused by an unreasonably dangerous product may be based on **breach of express warranty**. The defendant is **any person** who releases the product into commerce.

The plaintiff must prove 1) the defendant **made express warranties** about the product, 2) there was a **reliance** on the warranties, 3) the warranties were **breached** and 4) the **failure of the product to perform** as warranted for its **intended use** made it unreasonably dangerous and **caused injury**.

--o0o--

A. Damages

Damages based on a claim of breach of express warranty can be **personal injury**, **property damage** and **economic losses**, if they are caused by reliance on the express warranties.

--o0o--

B. Proper Plaintiffs

In some States the plaintiff must be **the person that relied** on the warranties, or else a **close family** member or **friend** of the person that relied on the warranties. In other States the plaintiff can be **any person, natural or legal,** who could **foreseeably be injured** by the product, **physically or economically** at the time the express warranty was made.

--o0o--

C. Defenses

The plaintiff must give **prompt notice of injury** to the defendant. The defendant may argue that a **general disclaimer** limits liability for property damage, but Courts generally reject that defense in actions for personal injury. The defenses of **assumption of the risk** and **contributory or comparative negligence** are also defenses to a products liability claim based on express warranty.

> **For Example:** The clerk at Home Despot sells Homer a ladder saying, "This ladder holds up to 500 pounds." But the Home Despot bill of sale given to Homer says, "No oral warranty of any merchandise for any purpose or use." Homer is injured when he climbs the ladder and he weighs less than 500 pounds. The clerk's oral statement was an **express warranty.** Homer **relied** on the warranty and the **general disclaimer** would usually be ineffective in an action for **personal injury** based on a **breach of express warranty**.

7. Products Liability for Breach of Implied Warranty

If an unreasonably dangerous product causes injury when **used for its intended purpose**, but no express warranties were made, an action may be based on **breach of implied warranty** if the defendant is **a commercial supplier** who releases the product into commerce. If the defendant is not a commercial supplier there is no clear basis to argue any implied warranty was made.

The plaintiff must prove the product was **impliedly warranted fit for the use that caused injury**. That means the plaintiff must either show 1) the product was obtained for its **ordinary use**, or 2) that it was obtained for a **particular use known to the defendant.** In either case plaintiffs must present evidence they **relied** on the defendants' expertise in selecting the product for the particular use, the product was unreasonably dangerous for that use, and that reliance **caused injury**.

> **For Example:** Hawker, a commercial supplier, sells Bubba a ladder after Bubba stated, "I need a ladder that will hold my cousin, Zippy. He weighs 300 pounds." Zippy is injured when the ladder collapses. If Hawker does not expressly state that the ladder would hold 300 pounds he has made <u>no express warranty</u>. But if he sells the ladder knowing the

intended use, and that Bubba is relying on his expertise, he has sold it with an implied warranty that it is suitable for that use because he is a commercial supplier.

--o0o--

A. Damages

Damages based on a claim of breach of implied warranty are the same as for a claim of breach of express warranty: **personal injury**, **property damage** and **economic losses** caused by reliance on the implied warranties.

--o0o--

B. Proper Plaintiffs

As with a PL claim based on breach of express warranties, some States require the plaintiff to be **the person that relied** on the warranties or a **close family** member or **friend**. In other States the plaintiff can be **any person, natural or legal,** who could **foreseeably be injured** by the product, **physically or economically** at the time the express warranty was made.

--o0o--

C. Defenses

As with product liability claims based on breach of express warranties, the plaintiff must give **prompt notice of injury** to the defendant, and **assumption of the risk** and **contributory or comparative negligence** are affirmative defenses to a products liability claim based on implied warranty.

8. Strict Product Liability

A **commercial supplier** may be held **strictly liable** for **personal injury** and **property damage** caused by release of an unreasonably dangerous product into the stream of commerce in almost all jurisdictions under the holding first reached in *Greenman v. Yuba Power*. **No showing of fault is necessary**.

The **possible defendants** are those people **regularly engaged** in supplying some product (e.g. shampoo). Some Courts have refused to apply strict liability to the resale of **used goods**. Strict liability is NOT applicable to defendants that regularly engage in **providing a service** to patrons that tangentially use a product (e.g. beauty parlors that use shampoo on patrons.)

Under one view strict liability applies to any injury resulting from **reliance** on **misrepresentations** by any **manufacturer or seller** about the **quality** of a product. [18]

--o0o--

[18] Restatement Second § 402-B.

A. Damages

Only **personal injury and property damage** can be recovered. The prevailing view is that claims of **mental distress** require proof of physical injury. And generally **economic damages** (e.g. lost wages; lost profits) cannot be recovered upon this theory.

--o0o--

B. Proper Plaintiffs

The **possible plaintiffs** are all who might reasonably be expected to use or otherwise be injured by the product. **Causation must be proven** the same as with a negligence action.

--o0o--

C. Defenses

Assumption of the risk based on an **express agreement or waiver** is NOT considered a valid defense, but **secondary (voluntary) assumption of the risk** and **misuse of the product** for an **abnormal** and **unpredictable use** are valid defenses.

> **For Example:** Tom buys a ladder at Dick's store. Tom later sells the ladder "as is" at a yard sale to Harry. Harry is injured when the ladder collapses. Examination reveals the ladder collapsed because it was manufactured with a defect. Harry can bring an action against Dick based on strict liability in tort because Dick's "store" was a **commercial supplier** and the product was **unreasonably dangerous** due to the "hidden defect". Harry has no cause of action against Tom. He cannot sue for strict liability because Tom was not a commercial supplier. Tom was negligent when he sold the ladder. And Tom made no express or implied warranties when he sold the ladder "as is". Harry also cannot recover **economic damages** like "lost wages" from Dick's store under a strict liability theory.

9. Comparison of Product Liability Theories

Each of the four product liability theories has certain limitations and advantages.

- Actions based on **negligence** and **strict liability** can be brought if injury results from any foreseeable use or misuse of the product.
- Actions based on **breach of express warranty** require that an express warranty was made that caused the product to be used in a specific manner that was unreasonably dangerous.
- Actions based on **breach of implied warranty** can generally only be brought against a commercial supplier for injury caused by use of the product in the way it was intended to be used or the defendant knew the plaintiff intended to use it.
- Actions based on **strict liability** can only be brought against a commercial supplier and not for economic losses (lost profits; lost wages). But no fault needs to be proven.

Chapter 10: Defamation

A tort action for **defamation** is a claim that a **false statement of fact** by a defendant was **published** to others causing a **caused injury to the reputation** of the plaintiff. The **tortuous act** by the defendant is the making and publication of the false statement and the **tortuous result** is **damage to the plaintiff's reputation** which may cause loss of income.

1. Falsity

The plaintiff in a defamation action must allege the statement made by the defendant is **factually false**. If the defendant proves the allegation is true, the plaintiff loses. So it is often said "truth is a defense". But it is actually more of a **passive defense** because it attacks one of the legal elements the plaintiff has a burden of proving.

2. Factual Assertions

"**Defamatory statements**" are **assertions of fact** about plaintiffs that may damage their reputation in the community. Facts are things that can be proven with evidence. If a statement is one of opinion, rather than fact, there is no defamation. But statements of fact that are merely phrased as opinion are still statements of fact.

> **For Example:** Bob calls Mary stupid. That's his opinion; not a fact. If Mary sues Bob for defamation she is stupid (and so is her attorney). [19]

3. Defamatory

A **defamatory statement** can be almost any factual statement that will cause plaintiffs to lose standing within their "community". It does not matter that in some other circles it would complimentary or of little relevance. However a defamatory statement must be a statement of **fact** and cannot just be a statement of opinion.

4. Publication

For a defamatory statement to be actionable **it must be published** or conveyed <u>to at least one person other than the plaintiff</u>.

> **For Example:** Tom writes Dick a letter accusing him of dishonesty. Dick is outraged, shows the letter to all his friends and then sues Tom for defamation. Dick has no case because he is the one who "published" the letter, not Tom. If Tom did not tell anybody his opinion, Dick's reputation could not be damaged. The damage occurs when Dick shoots his mouth off.

---

[19] If you don't understand this you're an idiot, ugly and stink too! Insulted? So sue me.

5. Statements about the Plaintiff

For defamatory statements to be actionable **they must be about the plaintiff**. If the defendants' statements are **merely insinuations** that might or might not be about the plaintiff, the burden is on plaintiffs to prove the statements were **understood by listeners** to be about them because they subsequently suffered **monetary losses**. That is explained below.

If defamatory statements are **about a group**, rather than individuals, NO members of a **large group** can bring an action for defamation, even if the statement is about "all" members of the group. But if the defamatory statement is about a **small group** EVERY member can bring an action for defamation. Generally this is true, **even if the remark targets an unidentified portion** of the group.

> **For Example:** "Half the cops in this town are on the take," is actionable by ALL the cops in the town if the "town" is Podunk, Utah, but it is not actionable by ANY cops if the "town" is Los Angeles.

6. Privileged Statements

It is a common error for law students to believe all false statements that cause damage to a plaintiff's reputation are actionable. Many, many false statements are <u>absolutely privileged</u> and can never be the basis of a defamation action. Among these are statements in **judicial proceedings**, **legislative proceedings**, confidential statements **between spouses**, statements **instigated by** or **consented to by** the plaintiff, and **reports of public proceedings**.

> **For Example:** President Obama is giving a speech to the joint houses of Congress on health care reform and Congressman Klansman jumps to his feet and shouts, "You're a liar!" His statement is absolutely privileged.

False statements made in Court pleadings cannot be the subject of a defamation action. They may be the basis for an abuse of process or malicious prosecution action. But they are never the basis of a defamation action. **Abuse of process** and **malicious prosecution** are explained in Chapter 14.

> **For Example:** Tom and Dick have a traffic accident. Tom files a complaint saying Dick caused the accident by running through a red light. Dick files an answer denying fault and saying Tom was the one who ran through a red light to cause the accident. Obviously one of these guys is making a false statement of fact. If a jury concludes Tom caused the accident, do you think Dick can sue him for defamation? [20]

A **qualified privilege** is also recognized when a plaintiff is acting **without malice** and as **reasonably necessary** to protect his **personal interest**, the **public interest**, a **common interest**, or the **interest of a third party**. [21]

---

[20] If you answer "yes" to this question you should not be in law school.

[21] This is probably the <u>least understood</u> aspect concerning defamation.

For Example: Tom sees Dick leaving a store hiding merchandise under his jacket. Tom yells, "Stop that guy. He's stealing something!" It turns out Dick has bought and paid for the merchandise and is hiding it from his wife because he intended to surprise her. Since Tom acted without malice in a reasonably necessary manner, intending to protect the interest of the store, his statement is privileged and he cannot be liable for defamation.

7. Presumption of Damages

Plaintiffs in defamation actions have the **burden of proving** statements by defendants caused damage to their reputations. However, under the common law there was a **legal presumption** that certain types of defamatory statements were damaging to reputation. Those are called **defamation per se**. If a statement is **defamation per se**, the Court may award a money judgment to plaintiffs without requiring any further evidence they suffered injury.

Other defamatory statements that were are not so clearly damaging to reputation were called **defamation per quod**. If a statement was defamation per quod, the Court could not award a money judgment to the plaintiffs unless they presented convincing **evidence they suffered monetary losses** as a result of the statements.

For Example: Dan says, "Pete cheats at cards." If this is defamation per se the Court can award Pete a money judgment without any proof that this statement injured Pete's reputation in any way. But if this is defamation per quod Pete must present evidence he suffered monetary losses as a result of Dan's statement.

Whether statements are defamation per se or defamation pre quod depends on three factors:

- Whether statements are **insinuations** that have to be **interpreted by the listener** or **clearly defamatory statements about the plaintiff**;
- Whether the statements are **written** or **oral**; and
- The **subject matter** of the statements.

8. Insinuations

Under the common law **insinuations** that might harm the reputation of the plaintiff were **always defamation per quod** whether they are oral or written, and no matter what the subject matter might be.

Three types of "**insinuations**" were recognized by the common law: **innuendo, colloquium**, and **inducement**. There were fine-point distinctions between these terms that are hardly worth noting. It is the sort of hair splitting that wastes your time and is irrelevant to passing the Bar. [22]

The important point is that if defendants do not clearly identify the plaintiffs as the subject of their statements, or the statements do not clearly make factual assertions about the plaintiffs that would damage their reputations, they are "**insinuations**" and **defamations per quod** in all cases.

---

[22] If passing the Bar is not of concern you bought the wrong book.

9. Clear Defamations of the Plaintiff

If defendants make statements that clearly identify the plaintiff and allege facts that would injure the plaintiff's reputation, they are **clearly defamatory.** But whether they were **defamation per se** or **defamation per quod** depended on whether the statements are **libel** or **slander**.

--o0o--

A. Libel

A defamatory statement is **libel** if it is **written or recorded** in a manner that gives its damaging effects longevity. Under the common law a written defamatory statement about the plaintiff was **libel** and **libel was** always **defamation per se**, regardless of the subject matter.

--o0o--

B. Slander

A defamatory statement is **slander** if it is **oral or transitory** in nature so that the damaging effect soon dissipates. Under common law an oral defamatory statement about the plaintiff was **slander** but it was only **defamation per se** if it accused the plaintiff of one of the following four things:

- Having committed a **serious crime**;
- Having a **loathsome disease**;
- Engaging in **business or professional misconduct**; OR
- Engaging in **sexual misconduct**. [23]

Any **slander** regarding any other subject matter was **always defamation per quod**.

> **For Example:** Dan says, "Pete cheats at cards."
>
> - If this statement was **written** it was **libel** and **defamation per se** because "cheating" is dishonest and always a dishonorable act; but
> - If this statement was **oral** it was **slander** and **defamation per quod** because it does not accuse Pete of a **serious crime,** of having a **loathsome disease,** of **business or professional misconduct** or of **sexual misconduct**.

10. Burden of Proving Damages

If plaintiffs prove the elements of **defamation per se** the Court can award money judgments without any proof the plaintiffs suffered monetary losses. These are **general damages**. If the plaintiff also proves the statements caused monetary losses those are **special damages** and they can be awarded in addition. This is often phrased, "The plaintiff can get generals without proving specials."

---

[23] The mnemonic for this is CLUB=Crime, Loathsome, Unchaste, Business

If plaintiffs only prove the elements of **defamation per quod** the Court cannot award any damages at all until unless the plaintiffs prove the defamations caused monetary losses. Those are **special damages**. If plaintiffs do prove **special damages**, the Court can award **general damages** in addition to the special damages. But if plaintiffs fail to prove defamations per quod caused monetary losses the plaintiffs get nothing. This is often phrased, "The plaintiff must prove specials to get generals".

> **For Example:** Dan orally says, "Pete cheats at cards." This is defamation per quod. If Pete cannot prove Dan's statement cost him some money, he doesn't have a case.

11. *New York Times v. Sullivan*

New York Times v. Sullivan (*New York Times v. Sullivan* (1964) 376 U.S. 254) is the most famous case regarding defamation and should be cited and explained in every discussion of the issue. Prior to *New York Times* a false statement about the plaintiff was considered sufficiently "wrongful" that damages, **including punitives,** could be awarded for any statement **injurious to reputation**, based on a presumption of injury, without any proof of injury. Therefore, prior to *New York Times* "wrongfulness" was not an express element a plaintiff needed to prove as long as the statement was proven to be **false** and presumably **injurious to reputation**. In addition some State laws often allowed Courts to award **punitives** for defamation based on findings of **negligence** alone.

Because an action for defamation could be brought for almost any inaccurate statement, bringing (or threatening to bring) defamation actions was an effective way for powerful parties to silence social critics, stifle political opponents and oppress minorities.

In *New York Times* oppressed Black southern civil rights leaders published an appeal in the New York Times asking for contributions to support the civil rights movement. In response L.B. Sullivan, a Commissioner of the City of Montgomery in Alabama, sued the New York Times claiming he had been defamed by inaccuracies in the advertisement. One of the falsehoods was a claim that Black students were expelled from schools for singing "My Country 'Tis of Thee" when in fact they were expelled for singing "The Star Spangled Banner."

An all-White jury in Montgomery, Alabama, determined that these and other inaccuracies were about Mr. Sullivan and so injurious to his fine reputation in their upstanding community that he was awarded $500,000 in damages against the New York Times. The Supreme Court of Alabama refused to reverse the award.

Upon review the U.S. Supreme Court held that court actions and awards for defamation were unconstitutional infringements upon protected speech in violation of the 1st Amendment to the U.S. Constitution unless the statement at issue was so wrongful that it was, in fact, unprotected speech. But where the false statement is not sufficiently wrongful, it is protected speech that may not be casually infringed.

Further the Court held that **public figures** claiming to have been defamed must prove the defendants acted with **actual malice**. Because of *New York Times* every action for defamation now requires analysis of the nature of the plaintiff and the statement at issue.

--o0o--

A. Public Figures

Under *New York Times* a **public figure** claiming to have been defamed must prove the defendants acted with **actual malice**.

A **public figure** is a person who has **affirmatively acted to step onto the public stage**. This also described as having "**injected themselves into the public eye**", "**stepping into the public arena**", or some similar metaphor.

A plaintiff must affirmatively act to publicize themselves or enter the "public arena" before the defamatory statement is made to be deemed a **public figure**.

> **For Example:** Paris Hilton goes on TV and says, "I hope my boyfriend never forgets me!" That makes her a **public** figure.

--o0o--

B. Actual Malice

Actual malice means the defendant made a false statement **knowing it was false** at the time or else acted **with reckless disregard for the truth**. That means stating that something is true without any factual basis for knowing if it is true or not.

> **For Example:** Paris Hilton says, "I hope my boyfriend never forgets me!" Later Jimmy Fallon says, "Her boyfriend will always remember her because it burns every time he pees." If Paris wants to sue him for defamation she is going to have to prove he **knew** that was false and had **no factual basis** for saying it. And that is sort of hard to prove after the things (and guys) she has done, occasionally on videotape.

--o0o--

C. Matters of Public Interest

Cases following *New York Times* expanded on its ruling. Those subsequent cases created a rule of law that defendants speaking out about **matters of public concern** are not liable for defamation unless the plaintiff can prove they EITHER acted with **negligence** OR **actual malice** AND the statements caused actual damage, either special or general damages. In other words, damages will not be presumed, and the burden is on the plaintiff to present actual evidence the statements damaged their standing in the community.

Matters of public concern are issues that would be subject to discussion in the news media. So this rule effectively protects members of the news media from being liable for defamation unless they are negligent. In fact, members of the news media are the experts on what the public wants to read and hear about. So in any action against a media defendant this is the rule applied.

--o0o--

D. Punitive Awards

Cases following *New York Times* also held that Courts could not award **punitives** ("punitive damages") for defamation unless plaintiffs proved defendants acted with **actual malice**.

--o0o--

E. Other Defamations

If the plaintiff is **not a public figure**, the subject of the defamatory statement is **not a matter of public concern**, and **punitives were not being awarded**, all of the prior, traditional rules concerning defamation continued to apply after the *New York Times* decision was issued.

--o0o--

12. Retraction Statutes

The majority of States have "Retraction Statutes" that allow defendants that have made defamatory statements to limit or avoid liability by "retracting" their statements. This is strictly statutory, not a common law considerations. The statutes of the various States vary widely. And a substantial minority of States do not have any "retraction statutes" at all.

--o0o--

13. Trade Slander

Trade slander sounds like defamation but it is more properly considered to be a type of **unreasonable interference with prospective advantage.** Trade slander is explained in Chapter 13.

Chapter 11: Invasion of Privacy

Invasion of privacy is a general label for **four separate tort causes of action**:

1. **INTRUSION** into the plaintiff's peace and solitude.
2. **DISCLOSURE** of private facts about the plaintiff.
3. Portrayal of the plaintiff in a **FALSE LIGHT**.
4. **APPROPRIATION** of the plaintiff's likeness.[24]

The first two of these, **intrusion** and **disclosure**, violate the plaintiff's **right to be left alone.** The third cause of action, **false light**, is similar to defamation except that it involves a false "portrayal" of the plaintiff that causes <u>embarrassment or inconvenience</u> instead of damage to reputation. These first three causes of action generally seek an award of **damages** but a demand for **legal restitution** is always possible. The last of these causes of action, **appropriation**, almost always seeks **legal restitution** rather than damages because the plaintiff seldom suffers actual injury.

1. Intrusion

A cause of action for **intrusion** arises when the defendant **unreasonably violates** the plaintiff's right to be left alone. The plaintiff must have a **"reasonable expectation of privacy"**. [25] That often means the right to be left alone in a private place. But the cause of action does not necessarily require a trespass onto private land. The intrusion may be by "spying", photographing, telephone calls, stalking, eavesdropping, etc. The key element is the defendant's acts must be **unreasonable**. The action may seek either an award of **damages** or **legal restitution**.

A **passive defense** to an action for intrusion is that the acts of the defendant were **not unreasonable** because the plaintiff **did not have a reasonable expectation of privacy**.

> **For Example:** Guido takes a picture of the Duchess of York lying naked on a public beach having her toes sucked, and sells it to the tabloids. Guido is NOT liable if it was in a place where the Duchess had **no reasonable expectation of privacy**.

An intrusion action may be based on unreasonable acts in public places harassing the plaintiff.

> **For Example:** After Ben rejects his romantic advances, Jerry rents a billboard across the street from Ben's apartment with the message, "Ben I love you! Will you marry me?" Jerry is evicted by the landlord. Jerry is liable for **intrusion** because he has acted unreasonably to deny Ben his **right to be left alone**, even though the acts were done in a public place.

2. Disclosure of Private Facts

An action for **public disclosure of private facts** arises when the defendant **unreasonably reveals embarrassing, private facts** about the plaintiff. [26] There is NO cause of action if the facts are **public facts**.

---

[24] If you rearrange these you can get a mnemonic of FLAID (or maybe LAID or FAID.... Imagination runs wild.)
[25] This may be called "intrusion of privacy" or some such.
[26] This may just be called "disclosure".

The "tortuous act" is the disclosure of the private facts, and the injury to the plaintiff is the embarrassment caused by the disclosure. But the action may also seek **legal restitution**.

Bear in mind that all arrest records, criminal prosecutions and most civil actions are matters of public record. So all your past DUI records, divorces, paternity suits, mug photos, etc. from your wayward youth can always be posted on the internet and shown to your neighbors and there is nothing you can do about it. But medical records are almost always **private records**.

> **For Example:** Bob reveals Linda's medical records out of malice. Bob is liable because these are private facts.

It has been argued (perhaps by members of the news media) that private facts concerning **matters of public concern** or **newsworthy events** can be disclosed, but there is no Constitutional basis for that argument. Nothing in *New York Times* or its progeny says any such thing.

> **For Example:** National Inkwire bribes Nurse Nancy for medical records showing Governor Wastrel caught the clap from his mistress. Nurse Nancy is liable for disclosing the records and National Inkwire will be too, if it publishes them.

3. False Light

An action for **false light** arises when the defendant makes **false (inaccurate) assertions**, express or implied, about the plaintiff, or else **falsely portrays** the plaintiff's **condition, beliefs** or **behavior** in a manner that caused the plaintiff **embarrassment** or **inconvenience**.

False light differs from defamation in that the false "assertions" or false "portrayals" are <u>not damaging to reputation</u> and actually may be flattering or intended to elicit sympathy.

> **For Example:** The National Inkwire falsely states, "Friends report that Michael Fish no longer has Parkinson Disease." That false statement does not damage Mr. Fish's reputation in any way. So there is no basis for bringing a defamation action, and the only possible cause of action is false light.

If a false statement about the plaintiff is damaging to reputation, the only cause of action suggested is defamation, <u>not false light</u>. If the statement is not damaging to reputation, the only cause of action is false light, <u>not defamation</u>. So the only possible situation when a plaintiff should plead both causes of action is when the statement is false and only "arguably" damaging to reputation. [27]

The "tortuous act" in a false light action is the defendant's false portrayal of the plaintiff, and the **damages** sought are compensation for the plaintiff's embarrassment or inconvenience. But the plaintiff may also seek **legal restitution**. *New York Times* has NO application to an action for false light and the plaintiff does not have to prove the defendant acted with malice.

---

[27] And that is the only situation when you should discuss both causes of action on an exam. Otherwise you are revealing your ignorance.

4. Appropriation of Likeness

An action for **appropriation** arises when the defendant uses the plaintiff's **name**, **voice** or **likeness** for **commercial or political purposes** without consent. This is almost always in the form of an advertisement, political statement or "public service announcement."

Merely using a photograph or recording of the plaintiff in a **public setting** without implication that the plaintiff endorses or has consented to be associated with a particular product or political cause, is NOT enough to support an appropriation action.

> **For Example:** National Inkwire publishes a picture of Bubba drinking beer on the beach above a statement that says, "More Americans Suffering from Obesity." Bubba has no cause of action for **appropriation** because the picture is not part of an advertisement and does not imply that Bubba favors any particular product.

The misuse of the plaintiff's likeness <u>does not have to be deliberate</u> and can arise from an innocent mistake.

Usually the plaintiff in an appropriation action seeks **legal restitution** to **prevent unjust enrichment** by the defendant rather than **damage**, because the plaintiff usually suffers little injury compared to the benefits enjoyed by the defendant. Restitution would be measured by the <u>larger</u> amount of 1) the **profits** the defendant gained from using the plaintiff's likeness or 2) the **costs the defendant avoided** by using the plaintiff's likeness without consent.

> **For Example:** Budweiser uses a photograph of Pete drinking Budweiser beer, without Pete's consent, above a statement that says, "Drink Budweiser, it's the greatest!" Budweiser is liable to Pete for **appropriation** because the advertisement **uses Pete's image to sell beer** and **implies that Pete endorses** Budweiser. Restitution damages would be calculated as the <u>larger</u> of 1) the **profit** Budweiser received from beer sales because of the advertisement, or 2) the **costs avoided** by using Pete's picture without paying him. [28]

---

[28] In a similar case Nestle used the picture of a California man (a professional model) on jars of instant coffee around the world for several years in numerous countries without securing his consent. He had been paid a "sitting fee" of $300 to pose for the photos, but had never been paid for or consented to the use of the photos. Nestle had no knowledge that the model had never consented to the use of the photos. It eventually was ordered to pay him over $5 million based on a portion of the worldwide sales of instant coffee with his picture on the label. What a tortuous wrong. Sure glad that didn't happen to me.

Chapter 12: Nuisance

A **nuisance** action seeks compensation for injuries caused by **unreasonable interference to property rights**. There are two types of actions for nuisance, **private nuisance** and **public nuisance**.

- A **private nuisance** is an **unreasonable interference** with the plaintiffs' ability to **use and enjoy** their **land**.

- A public nuisance is an **unreasonable interference** with the plaintiffs' ability to **use and enjoy public rights or resources**.

1. Unreasonable Conduct

An action for nuisance arises from **unreasonable conduct** by the defendant. It may be **intentional conduct**, done deliberately to interfere with the plaintiff's rights. Or it may be **negligent** conduct that accidentally interferes with the plaintiff's rights.

> **For Example:** Stoner plays music so loud it can be heard blocks away. His next-door neighbor, Tenant, cannot sleep at night. Stoner ' behavior is **unreasonable**, whether he intentionally acts to irritate Tenant or is just stoned. [29]

Unreasonable conduct must be **volitional** conduct.

> **For Example:** Zonker snores so loud it bothers his next-door neighbor, Tenant. Zonker's behavior is **not unreasonable** because it is not even a volitional act. [30]

2. Substantial Interference

The unreasonable conduct by the defendant must **cause substantial interference** with the plaintiff's exercise of his or her rights. The conduct must be of a type that it would cause disturbance to an **average reasonable person**. There is no basis for an award if the interference is caused by the **hypersensitivity** of the plaintiff.

> **For Example:** Farmer raises minks on his land. Rusty lives next-door, and when he plays country and western music the little minks get sad and drink themselves to death. Rusty's conduct is **not unreasonable** or a cause of **substantial interference** because Farmer's loss is the result of his minks' hypersensitivity (and lack of music appreciation.)

---

[29] When I was going to graduate school the dude who lived below my apartment frequently got really stoned and played his stereo super-loud. But if I asked him to turn it down he was always apologetic and compliant. It was unreasonable behavior, and a nuisance, but not an intentional act. Peace.

[30] In Davis, California, where there seem to be a lot of odd lawsuits over toads, potholes and such, a home-owner sued his next door neighbor recently because she snored. Maybe there are just some odd lawyers practicing there.

3. Standing

To bring an action for **nuisance** the plaintiff must have **standing** based on **injury suffered.** The requirements for standing are different between public and private nuisance.

--o0o--

A. Standing for a Claim of Private Nuisance

An action for **private nuisance** can only be brought by plaintiffs that have been **denied the use and enjoyment of their own land**. The plaintiffs may be **landlords, owners** or **occupiers** (tenants) of the land.

--o0o--

B. Standing for a Claim of Public Nuisance

An action for **public nuisance** may be brought by a **public official** on behalf of the public or by a **private plaintiff** that has been **denied the use and enjoyment of public rights or resources** in a **different way or to a greater extent** than other members of the public. If the plaintiff has suffered no different injury than any other "average" member of the public, it is the responsibility of public authorities to take action, and the plaintiff has no standing to bring an action.

> **For Example:** Moon-doggy brings a public nuisance action against Exxon because its oil tanker ran aground and fouled his favorite surfing beach. Moon-doggy has **no standing** because even though **the beach is a public resource**, he is not suffering a **different kind of injury** or a **worse injury** than any of the rest of the surfers that use the same beach.

4. Nuisance Compared to Trespass to Land

A nuisance action may arise out of trespass to land, but there must be **continuing acts of trespass** for the interference to be unreasonable and substantial. But an action for trespass to land can be brought if there is even a single intentional act. So an action for trespass to land may be possible when an action for nuisance is not.

But a nuisance action can be brought for **noises, vibrations, smells** or **lights** while a trespass action cannot because there is no physical entry onto the land.

So each cause of action may be possible when the other is not, depending on the facts.

5. Defenses to Nuisance

If an action for nuisance is based on a claim of negligence the defendant can raise a claim of contributory or comparative negligence as a defense. But the most common defense to a **private nuisance** action is "**coming to the nuisance.**"

"Coming to the nuisance" means that the conduct complained of already existed **when the plaintiff moved to neighboring land**. In a minority of states this is a **complete bar** to a negligence action. In most states this is merely a **factor of consideration** in **balancing** the reasonableness of the defendant's use of land against the interference caused the plaintiff, but NOT a complete bar.

> **For Example:** Sneezer keeps 400 cats in his house. Newcomb moves in next-door. Obviously this causes problems. Newcomb came to the nuisance but the court would find in his favor because Sneezer's use of the land is totally unreasonable by any measure.

6. Nuisance Remedies

Plaintiffs prevailing in nuisance actions have a **legal right** to award of a money judgment. It may be for **damages** caused by the unreasonable acts of the defendants, or it may be for **legal restitution** to prevent plaintiffs from reaping an **unjust enrichment** from their wrongful acts.

If an award of a money judgment would be an inadequate remedy the Court has discretion to grant equitable relief which would usually consist of an injunctive order stopping the defendant from continuing behavior that constitutes a nuisance.

--o0o--

A. Money Judgments as Nuisance Remedies

1) Damage awards for nuisance

The proper measure of a money judgment for **damages** caused by a nuisance depends on whether the nuisance was for a **temporary** period of time or will be a **permanent** condition.

- Damages for a **temporary nuisance** are measured by the monetary value of the **loss of use** suffered by the plaintiff during the period the nuisance existed;
- Damages for a **permanent nuisance** are measured by the **diminution of property values** caused by the nuisance.

> **For Example:** Owen's house is worth $40,000. Waist Management locates a toxic waste dump adjacent to it creating fumes that make it impossible for him to enjoy use of his land. If the nuisance was **temporary** Owen has a legal right to award of a money judgment to compensate him for the **loss of use he suffered** during the period the dump was in operation. If the nuisance is permanent (because the Court will not order the defendant to close the waste dump and restore the land) it is a **permanent nuisance**. In that case Owen has a **legal right** to a money judgment in the amount his **property value was permanently reduced**.

2) Legal restitution for nuisance

The proper measure of a money judgment in **legal restitution** is the amount necessary to prevent the defendant from reaping an **unjust enrichment**.

> **For Example:** Waist Management saves $1 million by locating a toxic waste dump next to Owen's home instead of putting it where it would not harm anybody. Owen has a right to

demand **legal restitution** in the amount of $1 million because that is the amount Waist Management saved by its wrongful act. Otherwise Waist Management will **reap an unjust enrichment** by deliberately injuring him.

--o0o--

B. Equitable Remedies for Nuisance

Nuisance causes of action frequently involve **pleas for injunctions**, **equitable remedies**, because legal remedies are often inadequate to compensate the plaintiffs for the loss of their ability to enjoy their land or public resources.

Before granting an injunction the Court must **balance** the interests of the plaintiff against the interests of both the defendant and **third parties** such as the members of the community who will be affected. In many cases the Court will **condition a grant of injunctive relief** on cooperation by the plaintiff.

> **For Example:** Dumpy has a large pile of discarded tires on his rural land. Newcomb builds a house next to the pile. Then Newcomb sues for nuisance because the tires are unsightly. The Court may order Dumpy to remove the tires on the condition that Newcomb must reimburse Dumpy for the costs because Newcomb came to the nuisance and no doubt paid less for his property initially because it was next to the tire dump.

The Court may refuse to enjoin a nuisance, allowing it to continue, on the condition that the **defendant reimburses the plaintiff for reduced property values**. This may occur when enjoining the nuisance would cause an inequitable impact on the defendant or third parties, yet an award of a money judgment to the plaintiff may go uncollected, allowing the defendant to continue a wrongful act with impunity.

> **For Example:** Quarry is a small gravel operation near Owen's house. Over time Quarry grows to be a $30 million operation employing 300 workers. Owen is subjected to increased dust and noise so he seeks an injunction to shut down Quarry. The Court may deny the injunction because shutting Quarry down would negatively affect both the workers and the community. But award of a money judgment to Owen may be an inadequate remedy because he may never be able to collect on it. So the Court may **conditionally deny** the injunction request by Quarry on the condition that Quarry reimburses Owen for the decrease in his property values. That assures that Owen is compensated without injuring any other parties.

--o0o--

C. Punitives for Nuisance

The Court may award **punitives** (punitive damages) for intentional nuisances.

> **For Example:** Sid deliberately plays music loud to irritate his neighbor, Wendy. The Court may award Wendy **punitives** to punish Sid for his acts.

Chapter 13: Malicious Interference

An **interference** action seeks compensation for **acts and statements** by the defendant that cause unreasonable interference to the plaintiff's **economic activities** such as business ventures, employment, contracts, and sales of property. There are three general types of unreasonable interference that give rise to this cause of action: **injurious falsehoods, interference with contract** and **interference with prospective advantage**.

1. Injurious Falsehood

An **injurious falsehood** is a false statement of fact made with malice that is published by the defendant and causes the plaintiff financial losses or gains the defendant an unjust enrichment.

The plaintiff must prove the defendant's statement is **false** and made with malice. **Malice** requires proof the defendant **disparaged** the plaintiff's business, property or financial interests with false statements **to injure the plaintiff** or **gain unjust enrichment**.

> **For Example:** Tom tells Dick he has decided to buy Blackacre from Harry. Dick falsely states, "Bad idea! Blackacre is on top of a toxic waste dump. Buy Whiteacre from me instead." This causes Tom to buy not buy Blackacre. Dick is liable to Harry for injurious falsehood because the statement was **false,** made **knowingly** for the **purpose** of benefiting himself and injuring Harry.

2. Interference with Contracts

The law seldom regards contract breaches to be tortuous acts. But it regards **encouragement of a breach of contract** or other **meddlesome interference** by a third party to be a tort.

Interference with contract is the act of **intentionally, and knowingly encouraging** a party to **breach an existing contract** or other **meddlesome interference**. The plaintiff is a contract party seeking **damages** for the injury caused by the interference or **legal restitution** for **unjust enrichment** gained by the defendant.

The plaintiff must prove the defendant was **aware a contract existed** and **intentionally interfered** with the contract relationship for **improper motives**. Improper motives would be **spite, malice**, to **gain advantage**, or **officious intermeddling**. The plaintiff must prove the interference caused **monetary losses** or that the defendant reaped an **unjust enrichment**.

> **For Example:** Disney agrees to pay Oliver $1 million to act in a film. MGM learns of the contract and offers Oliver $2 million to breach the contract with Fox and appear in its film instead. MGM is liable to Disney for interference with contract, for the larger of the **damages** Disney suffered as a result or the **unjust enrichment** MGM enjoyed.

There is **NO interference with contract** if defendants encourage **legal rescission** of existing contracts or avoidance of proposed contracts for reasonable business or personal motives.

For Example: Bo is a salesman for Sam's Used Cars under an **at-will contract** they can **legally rescind** at any time. Max, the owner of a competing car lot, approaches Bo and offers to pay him a higher salary. Max is not liable for interference with contract because **he has not encouraged Bo to breach a contract**. He has encouraged Bo to **legally rescind** a contract, and he is acting for legitimate business reasons.

3. Interference with Prospective Advantage

Interference with prospective advantage is a general term for a wide range of acts by a defendant that **intentionally and improperly interfere** with the affairs of a plaintiff **causing financial losses**.

In most States the plaintiff must prove the defendant **intentionally acted with improper motives** and/or in an **improper manner.** Some Courts have held that **negligence** alone may be sufficient if special circumstances indicate "moral blame". Improper motives would be for purposes of **spite, malice** or **unfair competition.** Improper means may include **picketing, boycotts, threats, violence** or **misrepresentation**. The plaintiff must prove **financial losses** or **unjust enrichment**.

"Trade slander" is a particular type of interference. It means unreasonable acts interfering with the plaintiff's business operation by picketing and/or distributing flyers, emails and other messages criticizing the plaintiff's business practices and products. If false statements are made, trade slander more closely resembles **injurious falsehood**.

For Example: Tom, owner of Tom's Café, pays Dick, a homeless man, to go into his competitor's restaurant, Harry's Café, and yell, "Oh, My God! I just found a finger in my chili!" Tom is liable to Harry for interference with prospective advantage. But since the statement was false it also suggests injurious falsehood.

The right of free speech is not unlimited. As explained earlier, a person is privileged to make statements, even false statements, BUT they must be acting reasonably to <u>protect their own interests</u> (or a third person's interest or the public interest) and <u>without malice</u>.

For Example: Bo buys a used car from Sam's Auto Sales and is not happy with it. Out of spite Bo paints his car yellow and parks it front of Sam's dealership with a sign that says, "I bought this LEMON at Sam's. Don't be a sucker like I was." This is not **reasonable** behavior. Bo should file a contract action. Sam can bring an action against Bo for **trade slander**, a type of interference. If he cannot prove he has suffered damages he can seek an **injunction** in equity to stop Bo from continuing this unreasonable behavior. [31]

"Slander of Title" is a particular type of interference. It means filing groundless **liens** or making **frivolous claims** against the **real property** of the plaintiff out of spite, malice or to gain an unjust advantage.

---

[31] This exact scenario actually occurred years ago in Norman, Oklahoma. The Court enjoined the defendant.

Chapter 14: Abuse of Process and Malicious Prosecution

Actions for **abuse of process** and **malicious prosecution** seek compensation for **improper use of the judicial system** to injure the plaintiff.

- **Abuse of process** is the act of starting or continuing a civil proceeding or criminal prosecution for a **malicious or improper purpose** causing injury to the plaintiff;

- **Malicious prosecution** is the act of starting or continuing a criminal prosecution for improper motives and **without probable cause** causing injury to the plaintiff.

Abuse of process relates to both civil and criminal actions and the key element is a **malicious or improper purpose**.

Malicious prosecution only relates to criminal actions and the key element is the **lack of probable cause**.

1. Abuse of Process

An action for **abuse of process** is a claim the defendant **started** or **continued** a **civil or criminal** proceeding for an **improper motive**, out of **ill-will**, and **without an honest belief in the merits** of the case or for **a purpose other than the claims in the complaint,** causing **injury** to the plaintiff.

> **For Example:** To prevent her ex-husband Bruno from getting visitation rights with little Junior, Buffy falsely tells the divorce court judge Bruno has been sexually molesting him. Buffy is using a civil proceeding for an improper purpose, the tort of **abuse of process**.

If an abuse of process action claims a civil action was filed for an improper motive, **special damages** must often be proven. But special damages do NOT generally have to be proven in the case of wrongful criminal prosecution.

2. Malicious Prosecution

An action for **malicious prosecution** is a claim that the defendant **maliciously started** or **continued** a **criminal** proceeding against the plaintiff **without an honest** and **reasonable belief probable cause existed**, causing **injury** to the plaintiff.

Malice can be **inferred from lack of probable cause**. This may be shown where the action **terminated** in a **favorable manner consistent** with the defendant's claim of **innocence**. The termination can be a **dismissal, acquittal** or **voluntary abandonment** of the prosecution.

The termination can NOT be a **compromise** or **involuntary abandonment** for lack of jurisdiction.

The plaintiff may bring the action for **malicious prosecution** even if there has been **NO final determination** of innocence, as long as the plaintiff has not yet been "re-arrested".

The defendant may claim **in defense** that proper motive and/or probable cause were not lacking because:

1) The plaintiff was, in fact, **guilty of the crime** in spite of the fact the plaintiff was acquitted,
2) The defendant **acted upon the advice of counsel**,
3) The defendant had an **honest and reasonable belief** in the truth of his accusation, or
4) The plaintiff **was convicted** of the crime and then obtained a reversal upon appeal.

> **For Example:** A North Carolina district attorney charges four college students from Duke University with raping an exotic dancer based on her claims. Nothing about that was improper because her claim created probable cause. But then he receives lab test results that prove the "victim" had sex with other several other men at the same time of the alleged "rape", and there is no evidence she had sex with any of the defendants. At that point there was no probable cause and his legal duty was to drop the charges. Instead he appeared on television continuing to accuse them of the crime, and he continued to pursue prosecution. That is **malicious prosecution**.

Chapter 15: Deceit, Concealment, Nondisclosure and Misrepresentation

Actions for **deceit, concealment, nondisclosure** and **negligent misrepresentation** are claims that defendants **intentionally or negligently misled** plaintiffs as to material facts.

- **Deceit** (also called **fraud**) is a **deliberate assertion of false facts, knowing they are false,** and **intending to induce** the plaintiff to rely on the assertion;

- **Concealment** is a **deliberate concealment of material facts intending to mislead** the plaintiff;

- **Nondisclosure** is a negligent **failure to disclose known material facts in breach of a duty** to reveal them; and

- **Negligent misrepresentation** is a negligent **assertion of false or incorrect facts.**

Each of these causes of action share common elements of proof as explained below.

1. Misrepresentation of Material Facts

Plaintiffs claiming deceit, concealment, nondisclosure or negligent misrepresentation must prove defendants **intentionally or negligently** misled them about **material facts** causing injury or giving the defendants an unjust enrichment. **Facts are material** if a **reasonable person** would consider them **important to a decision** whether to enter into a transaction or otherwise act based on the information.

--o0o--

A. False Promises as Statements of Fact

A **false promise** is a misrepresentation of a material fact when it **misrepresents the present intentions** and **state of mind** of the defendant, and those facts are important for the plaintiff to reach an informed decision whether to enter into a transaction or otherwise act. False promises given in exchange for consideration support causes of action for both deceit and breach of contract.

--o0o--

B. False Statements of Opinion

False statements of opinion MAY be a false material statement of fact if **special facts** show the defendant gave the statement **to induce** the plaintiff's reliance and the plaintiff's **reliance was reasonable** because of an **unequal access to information** between the parties.

--o0o--

C. Misrepresentation by Conduct

Misrepresentation may be by **word or conduct**. And it may consist of **total lies, half-truths, truths told in a deceiving manner, acts to conceal the truth,** or by **concealment when there is a duty to reveal** material facts.

2. Deceit Requires Scienter

As a general rule, in actions for **deceit**, the plaintiff must prove **scienter**. Scienter means that the defendant acted with **knowledge of the falsity** of the representations made to the plaintiff **intending to induce** reliance. Scienter is shown if the defendant:

1) **Deliberately lied,**
2) Made statements of fact **believing them to be false,**
3) Made statements as fact while **consciously ignorant** of the truth,
4) **Acted to conceal** the true facts,
5) **Acted to prevent revelation** of true facts or
6) **Deliberately breached a duty to reveal true facts** for the purpose of concealing the truth.

There is NO scienter if the defendant made misrepresentations of fact while **believing them true** and **believing there was sufficient information** to support that belief.

3. Intent to Deceive

An action for **deceit** requires proof the defendant acted intentionally **to deceive** or else intentionally did not act in breach of a duty to act **to deceive**. But, the intent does not necessarily have to be for a wrongful purpose or for personal benefit.

4. Reasonable Reliance

Plaintiffs in actions for deceit, concealment, nondisclosure and negligent misrepresentation must prove they **reasonably relied** on the defendant's misrepresentation of facts. **Reliance is NOT reasonable** if average reasonable people would not have relied on the defendant's representations.

> **For Example:** Ponsi tells investors he has a secret investment plan that will pay returns several times greater than other investment funds. No experienced investor would believe such claims, but **average people** who are not experienced investors might.

It is NOT a bar to an action if the plaintiff failed to investigate or investigated negligently. The plaintiff has NO DUTY to investigate the truth of a defendant's **deliberately false** statements.

> **For Example:** Shifty sells his car to Sucker by telling him it has new tires. After he buys the car Sucker discovers the tires are old and worn. Sucker's reliance is not **unreasonable** simply because he believed Shifty and did not investigate.

Reliance on **sales talk** (puffery), **predictions** of the future, or legal opinions by people without any legal training is not reasonable.

> **For Example:** Barfly tells Gullible, "You can't be arrested for drunk driving if you only drink beer." If Gullible knows Barfly has no legal training any reliance on his part is unreasonable and Barfly will not be liable for the consequences.

Reliance on **statements of opinion** is not reasonable UNLESS there are **special facts** to show the reliance was reasonable because of **unequal access to information** between the parties.

5. Right to a Remedy

Plaintiffs in actions for deceit, concealment, nondisclosure or negligent misrepresentation must prove they suffered **injury** or the defendants reaped an **unjust enrichment**.

Usually damages are **monetary losses** but injuries may include **personal injury** or **property damage**. **Monetary losses** can be measured by the **loss of expected benefits** or **out-of-pocket expenses** necessary to put the plaintiff into the position he was promised.

> **For Example:** Shifty sells his car to Sucker falsely claiming it has new tires. After Sucker buys the car he sees the tires are worn out. If it will cost Sucker $400 for new tires he can claim **damages** of the amount because that is what it will cost him to be put in the position he was promised.

--o0o--

A. Remedies Peculiar to Deceit Actions

In an action for **deceit** the plaintiffs may be awarded **general damages** (for distress and inconvenience) even if **special damages** (monetary losses, property damage, personal injury) are not proven.

Punitive damages may also be awarded to punish the defendants.

--o0o--

B. Remedies Peculiar to Negligent Misrepresentation

The MAJORITY of courts favor the **out-of-pocket** measure of losses when there is a claim for **negligent misrepresentation or negligent non-disclosure.**

General damages (for distress or inconvenience) generally are not awarded unless **special damages** are proven (monetary losses, property damage, personal injury).

No punitives are awarded for negligence.

6. Third-Party Plaintiffs for Deceit

Third-party plaintiffs can bring an action for **deceit** if the defendant acted with **intent to deceive them, intent to deceive someone else** or **should have foreseen they could** be deceived, even if the defendant acts without knowledge of the identity of the third-party plaintiff. [32]

> **For Example:** Tom tries to sell Dick his house by falsely claiming it has a new roof. Dick tells Harry about the house with a "new" roof. Harry buys the house based on that misrepresentation. Tom is liable to Harry for deceit, even though Tom tried to deceive Dick and did not even know Harry at the time.

7. Nondisclosure Requires Duty to Reveal

Actions for **nondisclosure** require plaintiffs to prove the defendants breached a **duty to reveal** material facts. Generally, a seller of property has **NO duty to reveal material facts** to a plaintiff, even if the plaintiff is clearly acting under a false impression. However, there are **exceptions** to that general rule. Courts consider the following factors:

1. Certain **types of contracts** (e.g. prenuptial agreements) require full disclosure by statute;
2. The **relationship** between the parties (e.g. fiduciary, confidential) may require disclosure;
3. The parties' relative **ability to discover and understand** the facts;
4. The **defendant's class or status** (e.g. seller of real property, physician);
5. The **importance of the fact** concealed (i.e. the degree to which it affects value); and
6. **Conduct by the defendant** that encourages the plaintiff's mistaken impression.

As a general rule there is a fiduciary duty to reveal all material facts when:

1. A **fiduciary relationship** exists between the parties;
2. The defendant honestly makes an **untrue statement** and **later learns the truth**;
3. Actions or words of the defendant **create a false impression** in the plaintiff; or
4. The defendant is a **seller of real property**;

> **For Example:** Seller paints over rust spots on his car. Later Buyer offers to buy the car. Seller has a duty to reveal the rust damage because his acts have **created a false impression** the car is sound.

> **For Example:** Tom offers to sell his house to Dick. The roof is 6 years old, but Dick says, "The roof looks new." Tom knows the roof is not new but remains silent. Tom is NOT liable for deceit because he **did nothing to mislead** Dick and has NO duty to dispute Dick's opinion about whether the roof looks new or not.

> **For Example:** Tom offers to sell his house to Dick. Tom knows the house is built on a toxic waste dump. Tom has a duty to reveal this **concealed fact materially affecting value** even if Dick never asks, "Is this house built on a toxic waste dump?"

---

[32] This is effectively "transferred intent".

8. Negligent Misrepresentation Requires Duty to be Accurate

Plaintiffs claiming **negligent misrepresentation** must prove the defendants had **a duty to give them accurate information**.

The duties of defendants to give plaintiffs accurate information depends on whether the plaintiffs are only at risk of **monetary losses** or if they are at risk of **personal injury** and **property damage**.

--oOo--

A. Duty to Plaintiffs Risking Only Monetary Losses

Defendants only have a duty to give accurate information to prevent **monetary losses** if the defendant 1) is in a **business or profession that involves transmission of accurate data** and 2) **knows the information will be relied on** by others.

Defendants who breach a duty to provide accurate information in this case are only liable to the **parties given** the information and **third parties known to rely** on the data provided.

> **For Example:** Tom, a plumber tells Dick in good faith, "Harry has excellent credit." Harry actually has a terrible credit history. Dick loans money to Harry and Harry defaults. Tom is NOT liable to Dick for negligent misrepresentation because Tom is **not the business** of providing credit reports.

--oOo--

B. Duty to Plaintiffs at Risk of Personal Injury and Property Damage

Defendants have a duty to give accurate information to prevent **personal injury or property damage** if the defendant **knows or should know the safety of others is at risk.** The duty and liability is to the **person given** the faulty information and extends to all **foreseeable people put at risk**.

> **For Example:** Tom is driving a truck slowly up a mountain road, and he sees Dick following close behind. Tom negligently waives his arm signaling Dick that it is safe to pass, even though there is a curve ahead. Dick tries to pass the truck and collides with Harry's car when it comes around the curve. Tom is liable to both Dick and Harry for negligent misrepresentation because he **knew the safety of others** was at risk and **negligently gave faulty information**.

9. Negligence by Plaintiff Asserted as a Defense

Defendants in actions for negligent misrepresentation or negligent non-disclosure can raise **contributory negligence** or **comparative negligence** as a defense. In this case the burden is on the defendants to prove either that **no reasonable person would have believed** the defendant's representations **without taking reasonable steps** to determine their accuracy.

Chapter 16: Conclusion

This outline provides a simple and summarized explanation of the black letter law and bright line rules of **TORT** law.

Black letter law means statutes and basic rules of broad theoretical application. And **bright line rules** are those decisional rules or logical guidelines created by the Courts for the determination of close cases.

To make the explanation here simple and avoid unnecessary confusion some of the details and minor views have been ignored and avoided in this outline. But the foregoing reflects about ninety percent of everything you should know to succeed in law school, and more than enough explanation of the rules of law for you to pass any Bar examination.

Among the materials that have been excluded from this outline are legal theories that have been widely abandoned, extreme minority views, rare exceptions, fact-bound cases, history of the law's development, most cases, highly unusual situations and dwelling on subtle distinctions. These issues and concepts are either unnecessary for your legal education, OR your professor will direct them to your attention.

Each professor of law, in every subject, holds a keen interest in narrow areas of the law of personal interest. Frequently this interest is based on their own legal education or their experiences in the Courts. When your professor expounds on an area of law given summary treatment in this outline it will be necessary for you to consult authoritative reference materials such as hornbooks to gain a greater understanding.

If your professor is adamant about some theoretical concept or nomenclature note that proclivity and modify your explanation of the law as necessary to humor those proclivities. But, you will find the Bar examiners far less interested in such marginal issues and much more concerned with the breadth of your knowledge of the rules of law set forth herein.

Other than those cases where a professor demands further knowledge in a narrow area, the foregoing should be entirely sufficient to impart an adequate **understanding** of the **law of tort**. However, mere **understanding is NOT ENOUGH** for you to succeed. Law school and the bar examinations require **both understanding** and ability to **explain the application** of the **law to the facts and facts to the law**.

This outline is NOT written for the purpose of explaining to you how you should explain the law on your examinations. You are urged to consult Nailing the Bar's "**How to Write Torts Law School and Bar Exams (B)**".

Tim Tyler, Ph.D.
Attorney at Law
Sacramento, California

Index

I

J

L

M

N

O

P

R

(This page intentionally blank)